Tender Grassfed Meat

Traditional Ways to Cook Healthy Meat.

By Stanley A. Fishman

Tender
Grassfed
Meat

Traditional Ways to Cook Healthy Meat

Stanley A. Fishman

Published by Alanstar Games, 3000 Danville Blvd., #205, Alamo, CA 94507
grassfedmeat@sbcglobal.net

Book design and illustration by Keren Fishman
Edited by Keren Fishman
Proofread by Alan Fishman

ISBN: 978-0-9823429-0-9

Library of Congress Control Number: 2009906544

PRINTED IN THE UNITED STATES OF AMERICA

Dedication

This book is dedicated to the grassfed farmers and ranchers of America, whose wisdom, hard work, and courage have made it possible for us to have superior meat. Raising grassfed and grass finished animals is both an art and a science, and I have so much respect for those who do it well. These are the elite few, who do things the hard way to create the very best meat there is. My deepest thanks and admiration goes to every one of them.

Acknowledgements

A book may have one author, but many people contribute to its creation. This book would never have come to be without the inspiration, help, and knowledge provided by so many fine people. I have been truly blessed.

The following people have helped me in major ways:

My wife, Keren Fishman, my true love, my best friend, my editor, designer, typesetter, illustrator, enthusiastic appreciator of my cooking, and my muse.

My son, Alan Fishman, my toughest critic, and vigilant proofreader.

My good friend, Ken Pritikin, whose enthusiastic appreciation of my cooking really motivated me to learn more and cook better.

My good friend, Joel Harris, for his helpful advice.

My good friend, Mary Weisend, for her help and encouragement.

My dear departed friend, Pat French, who opened my eyes to a better way of eating and healing.

To the writers group, especially Martha Lee and Suzanne Bare, for their enthusiastic help and feedback.

To Danette Voegeli-Sidhu, for her very helpful feedback and ideas.

To John Wood of U.S. Wellness Meats, for so much helpful information.

To Mary Graese of Northstar Bison, for the useful knowledge she shared with me.

To Carlos Alfaro, the best and most knowledgeable butcher I know.

To one of the greatest people who has ever walked the earth, Dr. Weston A. Price, who learned the truth about nutrition and taught that truth.

To the founders of the Weston A. Price Foundation, Sally Fallon and Dr. Mary G. Enig, for teaching me the truth about food and nutrition, and for fulfilling Dr. Weston A. Price's last wish, "You teach, you teach, you teach!"

And I also want to express my gratitude to two very special organizations. To the Weston A. Price Foundation, for providing the best nutritional information available, for their courageous fight to keep good food available for all people, and for teaching the knowledge of Dr. Price. To the Price-Pottenger Nutrition Foundation, for preserving the knowledge of Dr. Price, and for teaching that knowledge.

Contents

Why I Wrote this Book

There is a myth that grassfed beef is tough. Grassfed beef is tough only when cooked wrong. This book is all about cooking it right. Cook it right, and it is tender and delicious. The meat itself has a deep, beefy flavor that is robust and satisfying.

The first grassfed beef I cooked sure was not tender. It was tough, so tough that it hurt my jaws when I tried to chew it. I had wanted to switch to grassfed beef for its health benefits, but how can you eat something you can't even chew? And why would you want to eat anything that tasted so bad?

Fortunately, I did not give up. I remembered a story my dad told me. It was 1923, on the Canadian prairie where he was born. He and his brother, ages 10 and 8, were taking a long train trip to stay with their grandparents. His father gave them ten dollars, which they were to use to buy food during the trip. The ten dollars was intended to buy all their meals for the long trip. The black cooks on that railway were famous for their skill in preparing steak, which was very expensive. My dad and his brother decided to use most of the money to order steak, even though it meant that they would have little food for the rest of the trip. The meat was fork tender, so delicious that my dad never forgot it. Eighty years later, as he was dying, he remembered that steak, and the memory brought a smile. That steak had to have been grassfed.

This meant that there had to be a way to cook tender, delicious grassfed meat. But how? Everything I knew about cooking meat had failed.

Being an attorney, I am accustomed to solving problems by researching and analyzing them. Since almost all the beef eaten by people throughout history was grassfed, I figured there must be a lot of grassfed cooking knowledge that was gained over time. I decided to ignore everything I had learned about cooking meat, and to learn from the people who had only grassfed meat to cook. I read literally hundreds of cookbooks and history books, finding thousands of descriptions of how people have cooked meat, as well as a staggering number of recipes. Most of this information was not practical for modern kitchens, but I got a lot of ideas. I combined, modified, experimented. I tried ideas and techniques from England, France, Poland, Germany, Hungary, early America, Ancient Rome, the Russian steppes, the Argentine Pampas, the Basque mountains, and many other countries and regions.

I began to produce tender grassfed beef, with great flavor, taste and texture. Properly prepared, the meat had a deep, rich flavor and was satisfying, leaving my family feeling good and refreshed after every meal. The taste was so good that we switched completely to grassfed meat. Even my teenage son, who originally wanted the meat he was used to, now prefers grassfed meat.

Much of what I have learned is in this book. You can prepare tender grassfed meat. Better yet, you can eat it and enjoy it.

Part 1:

How to Cook
Tender Grassfed Meat

The Different Kinds of Beef, or Why Grassfed Is Best

The conventional beef industry will tell you that all beef is the same, with the only difference being the grade given by the USDA, such as prime, choice, select, etc.

This is just not true. There is a huge difference between the different kinds of beef available.

- The taste is different.
- The way the cattle are raised, treated, and fed is different.
- The very composition of the meat and fat is different.
- The nutritional profile is different.
- The effect on your health from eating the meat and fat is different.
- The water content is different.
- And, they must be cooked differently.

These differences are huge. It is important to understand them so you can make a wise choice of which kind of beef to eat.

Three Very Different Kinds of Beef

I divide the beef available in the United States into three very different types:

- Factory Beef (also known as conventional beef)
- Grain Finished, Hormone and Antibiotic Free Beef
- Grassfed, Grass Finished Beef

After much study, the only beef I eat is grassfed, grass finished beef. These are the reasons why.

Factory Beef

This kind of beef did not exist before World War II. Yet it quickly became just about the only beef available in the U.S., and still comprises over 95% of the beef raised in the U.S.

Factory cattle are allowed to graze on pasture early in life, but are given large amounts of growth hormones and antibiotics. The combined effect of the hormones and antibiotics is to make the cattle put on weight and grow much faster. The antibiotics are given routinely, even if the animal is not sick. The vast majority of the antibiotics manufactured in the U.S. are given to cattle for this purpose.

The factory cow is sent to a feedlot for the last few months of its life. The cattle are crowded together in pens, and are not allowed to graze.

The cattle are fed a mixture which is calculated to make them grow at the fastest possible rate. The faster the cattle fatten, the more profitable they are. In addition to the growth hormones and antibiotics, they are fed corn, soybeans, grains, and animal byproducts. Most of this feed was grown with the use of pesticides.

None of these items are part of a cow's natural diet. Cows are ruminants, designed to eat grass, and other prairie and meadow plants. The grain feeding has another effect — it changes the very chemistry of the cow's stomachs, creating a more acidic environment that can cause digestive problems. Grain feeding also changes the ratio of omega-3 to omega-6 fatty acids to an unbalanced ratio with far too much omega-6. Grain feeding also greatly reduces the amount of CLA in the meat. CLA is a very beneficial nutrient which helps the body burn fat and avoid obesity.

The factory beef is delivered in various primal cuts to the supermarket. The meat is watery, often giving off much liquid. Because of the water, it is often cooked at very high heat, which can cause chemical changes in the meat. The beef itself has very little flavor, except in the fat, which is usually trimmed off. The meat shrinks substantially when cooked. This beef requires a lot of seasoning to be palatable.

The fat itself can contain pesticide residue from the feed. The meat can contain residues of the growth hormones that were given to the cow throughout its life. These hormones often mimic the effect of estrogen in human bodies. The meat can contain residue from the antibiotics that were pumped into the cow throughout its life. This antibiotic residue is believed to be an important factor in the development of antibiotic resistant bacteria. The American Medical Association has tried to get the practice of giving antibiotics regularly to healthy cows banned, for this very reason.

The U.S. government and the cattle industry state that hormone residues disappear after a certain amount of time. Not everybody agrees with that statement. I should mention that U.S. government agencies have found that conventional American beef is safe for human consumption. However, "safe" does not mean "best."

Properly cooked grassfed beef tastes much better than factory beef. In fact, it tastes so much better that I will never eat factory beef again.

Grain Finished, Hormone and Antibiotic Free Beef

This beef is far better than factory beef. Most of the organic beef raised in the U.S. is of this type. These cattle do not have growth hormones implanted in them, and are not given growth hormones in any way. They only get antibiotics when they are sick. Some programs will reject any animal that has ever had antibiotics. The best programs do not overcrowd the cattle, and treat them humanely. These cattle are fed on grass for the majority of their lives, often grazing on good pasture. When they are sent to a feedlot, they are fed a vegetarian diet, consisting of corn, soymeal, silage, and hay, often including barley and other grains, sometimes even potatoes.

If the beef is organic, the feed for the cows must be organic as well, which means it cannot have been sprayed with pesticides. Many non-organic producers avoid feed that has been treated with pesticides.

Grain finished beef does have its problems. Corn, grain, and soybeans are not the natural food of cattle. The meat is still too watery, and shrinks a lot in cooking. Most of the flavor is still in the fat. Despite these problems, grain finished, hormone and antibiotic free beef is a much better product than factory beef.

I used to eat a lot of this kind of beef. In fact, when I first thought of writing this book, I was going to devote a large section to recipes on grain finished, hormone and antibiotic free beef. I discarded that idea as I became better at cooking grassfed beef. Why?

Taste

Taste was the main reason. Good grassfed beef, when properly cooked, has a depth of flavor, a dense, meaty texture, a good clean mouthfeel that no grain fed beef can ever come close to. It just tastes better. Much, much better.

Nutrition

Cattle were never meant to eat grain. Feeding grain to cattle causes the amount of nutrients in the meat, such as CLA, to go down substantially. Feeding grain to cattle causes the fat in the cattle to become completely unbalanced with an excess of omega-6 fatty acids. Grassfed fat retains the proper balance between omega-3 and omega-6 essential fatty acids, which is very healthy. Omega-3s are in very short supply in the Standard American Diet (SAD).

Water Content

Feeding corn, grain, and soybeans to cattle makes their flesh much more watery than grass feeding. This water makes it much harder to cook the beef properly, requiring the use of very high heat and/or longer cooking times. The water dilutes the taste and ruins the texture of the meat.

Satisfaction

Good grassfed beef is satisfying and revitalizing. I feel renewed, stronger, and revitalized after eating grassfed beef. I have never felt this satisfaction after eating grain finished beef.

Grassfed, Grass Finished Beef

This is the kind of beef that was eaten for most of human history, for thousands and thousands of years. Done right, this is the best there is, in taste, in nutrition, in texture, in mouthfeel, in everything.

Taste

When properly cooked, grassfed, grass finished beef has tremendous flavor. The beef actually has its own robust, beefy taste, unlike factory beef, which has very little flavor outside of the fat. Grassfed beef has considerably less fat, which gives it a clean taste that is never greasy. The fat in grassfed beef has great flavor, and differs greatly in composition from factory beef.

Grassfed beef from each producer varies in taste and sometimes in cooking qualities. This is because the cattle vary in breed, the plants they eat vary, the soils the plants grow in vary, and there are other variables. The beef from every grassfed producer I have tried has its own distinct taste. Even beef from the same producer varies in taste during different times of the year, depending on how green the grass is. I enjoy this variety, as it provides many different tastes, all of them good, and some of them great. I will actually consider the distinctive taste of a particular producer's beef when planning a meal, much like someone might pick out a particular wine.

When properly cooked, grassfed beef is tender and delicious.

Nutrition

Grassfed beef is usually free of hormones, antibiotics, and other growth promotants. Since they only eat grass, their meat and fat do not contain residues of pesticides or growth hormones. The fat from grassfed cattle is full of healthy CLA and omega-3s. Our very cells need a good supply of omega-3s. Many people take fish oil supplements to get omega-3s. The fat profile of grassfed beef is similar to that of wild fish — in other words, lots of omega-3s.

Water Content

Grassfed beef shrinks much less in cooking because it is not full of water. This means that you have a lot more to eat once the meat is cooked. Because grassfed beef shrinks so much less, it is often more economical than other beef.

Satisfaction

The satisfaction that you get from eating grassfed beef has to be experienced to be believed. I feel satisfied, nourished, stronger, and happier, every time I eat grassfed beef. There was a traditional saying in Germany, "Beef gives strength." I never understood the truth of this saying until I ate grassfed beef.

CLA and Omega-3: Two Good Reasons to Go Grassfed

CLA is the common abbreviation for Conjugated Linoleic Acid. CLA occurs naturally in beef and milk. CLA has many health benefits. Various studies have shown that CLA:

- Increases the metabolic rate
- Increases muscle mass while reducing fat
- Decreases abdominal fat
- Strengthens the immune system
- Reduces the risk of cancer
- Reduces the risk of heart disease
- Reduces the risk of diabetes
- Reduces the risk of hyperthyroidism
- Normalizes thyroid function

The levels of CLA are much higher in grassfed cows than conventional cows. Cows eating green grass produce a lot of CLA.

Omega-3 is an essential fatty acid. Humans must have the right balance of omega-3 fatty acids and omega-6 fatty acids to be healthy. Unfortunately, the Standard American Diet (SAD) is totally unbalanced in favor of omega-6 fatty acids. Almost all Americans need far more omega-3 in their diet. The omega-6 excess has been associated with a greatly increased risk of cancer, heart disease, obesity, rapid aging, and many other problems. Many doctors advise their patients to take fish oil capsules to try to help with the imbalance.

Grain fed beef is totally unbalanced with an excess of omega-6 fatty acids.

Grassfed cows have a much higher level of omega-3. Grassfed and grass finished beef has the proper balance of omega-3 and omega-6 fatty acids.

A Humane Reason to Go Grassfed

It was one of the most beautiful pieces of grassfed meat I had ever seen, with a deep red color with tiny snow white flecks of marbling. I asked my butcher where he had found such a great piece of meat. The butcher, who had spent a lot of time on his aunt's cattle ranch in Mexico as a boy, said two words, "Happy cow." He went on to explain that a cow who had led a peaceful, happy life on pasture, and who was killed quickly, without fear, provided the tastiest and most tender meat. All the ranchers knew this.

Grassfed cattle spend their lives on good pasture, peacefully grazing, while eating the food they were designed to eat. They are together in a herd with other cows and have the social interactions normal for cattle. The wise grassfed rancher knows that the happier the cow, the better the meat, and does all that can be done to give the cows a happy, healthy, peaceful life.

Factory cows are confined in a feedlot for months, never allowed to graze, fed unnatural foods, and pumped full of hormones and antibiotics.

While I am convinced that humans have to eat meat to be healthy, that does not mean that the animals should be mistreated. I believe it is morally wrong to inflict any unnecessary suffering on meat animals. I believe it is morally right to support good and humane treatment of these animals.

More humane methods of slaughter have been developed and are typically used on grassfed cattle. Done right, this means the animal is killed by surprise, without fear or suffering.

Eating only grassfed meat is one of the best ways to support more humane treatment of meat animals.

What is Grassfed Beef?

The term "grassfed beef" is somewhat confusing, as all cattle receive some grass feeding. The United States Department of Agriculture has adopted a labeling standard as to what is "grassfed" meat. Under the standard, grassfed meat must come from a ruminant animal that has eaten only grass and forage. The animal may still be labeled "grassfed" if it has had milk before being weaned. The standard also prohibits the feeding of grain, or grain products, and requires that the animal has continuous access to pasture during the growing season. Unfortunately, the standard is silent as to the use of hormones and antibiotics.

"Grassfed beef" is generally understood to mean beef that has not only been raised on grass, but finished on grass. In other words, all that a grassfed cow should ever eat after weaning is grass and plants growing in the pasture. The cow should actually eat these plants in the pasture, while they are alive and growing. This is truly live food! Lush green grass of the proper height is best. In winter, it can be necessary to feed grass products such as hay and silage to the cows — but they should be eating good green grass in the pasture during the spring, summer, and fall. The beef is best when the grass is green. However, I have ordered and enjoyed excellent grassfed beef during the winter.

The grassfed movement has its own understanding of what is grassfed beef, regardless of government standards. True grassfed beef means no hormones, no corn, no soymeal, no animal byproducts, rendered or otherwise, no grain feeding, no subtherapeutic antibiotics, no crowded feedlots — just grass and forage.

It takes a great deal of knowledge and skill to raise good grassfed cattle. It is an art as well as a science, a craft comparable to that of an expert winemaker. It takes much longer for a grassfed cow to be finished that a factory cow. During this extended time, many actions must be taken by the rancher, and done right.

Fortunately, some ranchers have either retained the old skills or relearned them, and raise excellent grassfed beef. They have found breeds or crossbreeds that fatten well on grass, and have terrific flavor, when properly cooked.

The Cooking Advantages of Grassfed Beef

While I have read many articles on the health benefits of grassfed beef, I have never seen one on the cooking benefits of this wonderful meat. Grassfed beef has many advantages in cooking, once you know how to do it.

Grassfed beef is denser, and not nearly as watery as factory or grain finished beef. This has several advantages.

Less Shrinkage

Grassfed beef retains most of its volume when properly cooked with a dry heat method. In other words, there is very little shrinkage. In contrast, factory and grain finished beef shrink dramatically when cooked with a dry heat method (except at very low heat). For example, after you cook two pounds of grassfed beef, you have much more to eat than with two pounds of factory beef.

Browns Beautifully on Medium Heat

This allows you to brown a grassfed steak on medium heat, and to finish it on low heat. The lower heat makes it very easy to cook a steak to perfection. I typically sauté steaks in pastured or European style butter, which does not burn, and does not need to be clarified at this lower heat.

In contrast, watery factory beef can only be browned at very high heat, which is why so many steakhouses boast of their super-hot broilers (1700 degrees!) The extremely high heat required creates much smoke, and changes the very molecules of the meat. Butter will burn, and produce an unpleasant taste when superheated.

Does Not Release Water in the Pan

Factory beef and grain finished beef will release water into the pan when they are heated. This really interferes with the browning and searing process, and can ruin the taste and texture of the meat. It will also dilute any sauce or gravy. The only effective way to combat this is to use really high heat. Time and time again, I have read statements by gifted cooks from other lands who described their shock and dismay upon seeing the water gush out the first time they cooked American beef. Most grassfed beef will not do this. In fact, the only cut of grassfed beef I've seen release significant liquid was hangar steak, which is a very juicy cut.

Much More Satisfying

Grassfed beef is denser, and is much more filling. You are satisfied with less. Now that I eat grassfed beef, I eat half the amount of beef that I used to.

Cooks Much Faster

Grassfed beef just cooks faster. Much faster. This is because it lacks excess water and has less fat. This really saves time. You can cook a delicious roast in no more than 30 minutes in the oven.

Tastes Better, Thus Needs Less Seasoning

Grassfed beef, properly cooked, has great natural flavor right in the meat, as well as in the fat. Factory beef and grain finished beef have very little flavor in the meat, all the flavor being in the fat. Because of the great natural flavor, grassfed beef needs very little in the way of seasoning. The other beef needs all kinds of flavors and seasonings to be palatable.

An added bonus is that there is a definite variety in the taste of grassfed beef, depending on the breed of cattle, and depending on the grasses the cows graze on. These grasses vary between different parts of the country, so grassfed beef raised in Missouri tastes quite different from grassfed beef raised in the mountains of Idaho. They are both delicious, but the flavor is definitely different. This provides for a great variety of different tastes, which can be savored in the same way a wine lover appreciates different kinds of wine.

Bison Should Taste Like — Bison

I first tasted bison in the 1970's, at a restaurant called The Elegant Farmer, in Oakland, California. The steak that was served looked like a Porterhouse steak, but it did not taste like a Porterhouse. The medium rare bison was a deep red color, a deeper color than beef. The taste was nothing like beef. It was deep, rich, mild, and slightly sweet. It was wonderful. My friend had also ordered the bison steak, and he loved it. We ate at The Elegant Farmer regularly over the next several years. We always had the bison steak. This custom finally came to an end. Our steaks arrived. I took the first bite and tasted — beef. A few seconds later my friend loudly exclaimed, "This isn't bison, it's beef!" We called the waitress over. She checked with the kitchen, and assured us it was bison. We didn't believe her. The chef assured us it was bison. We didn't believe him. The manager assured us it was bison. We didn't believe him. It still tasted like beef. We left, convinced that the restaurant had tried to pass beef off as bison. We never returned to The Elegant Farmer. The restaurant is long gone, but the memory of the bison remains.

I believed for years that the restaurant had tried to pass beef off as bison. I was wrong.

My Quest for Good Bison

My next experience with bison came at a natural food store. The meat looked very different from the beef at the same counter, having a very different color. I happily bought a roast and some steaks, not even caring about the price. I made the roast for dinner that very night. I took the first bite and tasted — beef. I couldn't believe it. I was very disappointed. I made the steaks for lunch the next day. I carefully barbecued them, thinking that this method might bring out the bison flavor I remembered so well. I took the first bite and tasted — beef.

I returned to the store and talked with a couple of the butchers. I asked them why the bison tasted like beef. Both of them said that it was the way bison tasted.

I decided to look on the Internet to see if I could find bison that tasted like bison. I found a number of producers who sold bison over the Internet. They all emphasized how their bison was naturally raised, the health benefits of bison, and how good it tasted.

I ordered some bison and eagerly awaited its arrival. I cooked it carefully, thinking I was going to eat the real thing. I took the first bite and tasted — beef. That was it. I gave up.

A Clue

Several years later, I had my first taste of good grassfed beef. I noticed immediately that it tasted quite different from the beef I had been eating all my life. It occurred to me that maybe bison tasted like beef because of how they were fed. I researched the subject thoroughly on the Internet. While most bison producers emphasized how healthy the meat was and how naturally the bison were raised, they were pretty non-specific on how the bison were finished. It was not at all clear what the bison actually ate after the initial pasturage. I called several producers by telephone and discussed the matter with them. It became clear that they were finishing their bison on grain, soybeans, and "protein supplements."

The whole situation became clear to me when I read an article about raising bison. It stated that a decision had been made to have bison "taste like beef" because consumers were "used to" the taste of beef. This involved finishing the bison on grain, and giving them "protein supplements." The article also stated that the "protein supplements" were necessary for the bison to grow fast enough.

Mystery Solved

Finally, the mystery had been solved. Bison tasted like beef because bison were fed like cattle.

The solution was obvious, I had to find a producer who fed and finished their bison on the native grasses the bison were meant to eat.

I finally found a producer whose website made it clear that their bison were raised and finished on the native grasses, nothing else. I called the company to confirm this. I asked the nice lady on the other end of the line to describe the taste of their bison. She said it was deep, rich, mild, and slightly sweet. Those were the very words that I would use to describe the taste of the bison I had at The Elegant Farmer, so many years ago.

I quickly ordered some steaks. The steaks finally came. I cooked them carefully, and took the first bite. The meat was juicy and tender. It tasted deep, rich, mild, and slightly sweet. It tasted nothing like beef. It was bison, in all its delicious glory.

My quest had come to a successful end. The key to the quest turned out to be grassfed and grass finished bison.

I have found several producers who raise bison which taste like bison. (See *Sources*, page 217.) I salute them for their superb bison meat which tastes just like — bison.

The Different Kinds of Lamb, or Why American Grassfed and Grass Finished Is Best

As recently as the 1970s and 1980s, you could find magnificent, absolutely delicious American lamb right at the meat counter of a supermarket. The lamb was grassfed and grass finished, and had a superb flavor from high quality pastures. The lamb came from breeds that were raised for meat, not wool. Many lambs, especially in the West, were still raised by Basque shepherds, who knew how to raise superior lamb. While not all lamb was of this quality, much of it was. Sadly, those days are long gone.

The American lamb industry has thrown out quality for quantity and profit. Most American lambs are given grain and "protein supplements" that make them grow much faster. Unless the lamb is organic, the grain and supplements have been heavily sprayed with pesticides. The United States is almost the only country that feeds grain and "protein supplements" to lambs. In fact, American lambs are much larger that those raised in other countries. The average weight of an American lamb is no less than twice the average weight of lamb in many other countries. The American leg of lamb, which used to weigh between 4 to 5 pounds in the '80s, weighs between 7 to 10 pounds today. What is the result of this dramatic increase in size? The lamb industry tries to portray this as an advantage, citing "bigger chops." What they really mean is "bigger profits." Truth is, smaller lamb has always been considered tastier, having a milder flavor.

Lamb Tastes Like What It Eats

Lamb that has been raised and finished on a diet of natural grasses, perhaps including some wild herbs, develops a wonderful, natural flavor. Lamb that has been finished with grain and other supplements lacks flavor. It also has more fat, and actually tastes greasy. A rancher who raises grassfed lamb described the taste of conventional lamb as "a big, fat, greasy glob of nothing." I agree. No wonder most Americans do not like lamb. Even organic lamb of this type lacks flavor, as organic grain and soybeans are still grain and soybeans, and are still substances that no lamb was ever intended to eat. Finally, giving the lambs food they were never intended to eat reduces the amount of CLA in the meat, and reduces the omega-3s in the meat, greatly reducing its nutritional value. This kind of "lamb" can only be made somewhat palatable by the heavy use of flavoring marinades, sauces, and spices to disguise the lack of flavor in the meat. Why bother? I never use this type of "lamb."

Imported Australian Lamb

The United States imports a lot of lamb from Australia. While this lamb is supposed to be grassfed and grass finished, some grain may be used, though the amount is far less than that used in the U.S. The size of this lamb varies considerably. I have found the quality of imported Australian lamb to be very inconsistent. Sometimes I have picked up a tender rack of Australian lamb or some loin chops that had a great, mild flavor, and were absolutely delicious. I have also purchased Australian lamb, especially leg of lamb, that had a strong, gamy flavor that ruined the taste of the meat, and could be made palatable only through the heavy use of intense marinades, spices, and sauces. Some of it was quite tough. My guess is that some of this lamb came from breeds that were bred for meat, and some came from lamb that was bred for wool. Some of the lamb was fed some grain, and some of it wasn't. It is very hard to tell what the meat on the counter was fed and what breed it was.

Imported New Zealand Lamb

A lot of lamb is imported from New Zealand. This lamb used to be grassfed and grass finished. In the last couple of years, a switch in feeding practices occurred. It now appears that a large amount of New Zealand lamb that is imported to the United States is finished on grain, just like most American lamb. I no longer eat lamb from New Zealand.

American Grassfed Lamb

Fortunately, there are a number of ranchers who are raising American lamb the traditional way, grassfed and grass finished, on good unsprayed pasture. Many of these ranchers use breeds that were developed for meat, not wool. These lambs are usually smaller than the conventional lambs, though this varies with the breed and the producer. This kind of lamb can be absolutely wonderful and tender, with a mild, delicious flavor that is so much better than the other kinds of lamb. The natural grasses and herbs in the United States can give a wonderful flavor to lamb. Even people who think they hate lamb love this kind of meat. The flavor of this lamb needs no disguise, and is at its best with the use of traditional flavorings that bring out the great natural taste.

The recipes in this book were tested with grassfed and grass finished American lamb.

I cannot find this lamb at any store in my area, and have had to order it directly from the producer. (See **Sources**, page 217.) It is well worth the extra effort.

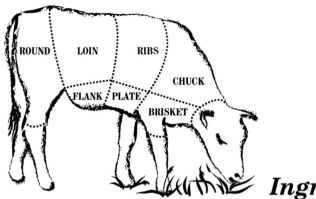

Ingredients

What You Need and Why

Recipes are not enough when it comes to making tender grassfed meat. You will need to forget just about everything you know about cooking factory meat, because grassfed is different. Grassfed meat does not respond well to artificial ingredients, or to artificial cooking methods, or non-traditional cookware. Grassfed meat tastes best with the natural ingredients used by traditional peoples, traditional cookware, and traditional cooking techniques. Many of these ingredients and techniques are impractical in our modern world, but I have developed modifications and substitutions that work.

To succeed in making tender grassfed meat, your kitchen and pantry must be prepared. This requires a certain amount of effort, but once it's done, it's very easy to maintain.

All fruits, vegetables, herbs, spices, oils, vinegars, and condiments should be organic, or the equivalent. But organic is not enough. There is a dramatic difference among various organic products. Some are wonderful, and some are worthless.

You need the right ingredients, these include:

- The right kind of grassfed meat

- The right kind of oil

- The right kind of animal fat

- The right kind of butter

- The right kind of salt

- The right kind of spices

- The right kind of condiments

- The right kind of organic vegetables, herbs, and fruits

- The right kind of broth

Cookware is also important. Many modern pots, pans, racks, and other cookware just will not work for making traditional grassfed meat.

And there are some great techniques that will help you cook tender grassfed meat.

When your kitchen and pantry are set up, you will be ready for the recipes, and some of the best, healthiest eating you have ever enjoyed.

Why Organic and Natural?

I call for organic vegetables, fruits, and spices in all of my recipes. You can also use the equivalent of organic, which is food that has been grown by organic methods, but has not received organic certification.

Organic foods are usually considerably more expensive, spoil much faster, and are often harder to find. So why use them? The simple answer is: because they taste better; because they work in my recipes; and because they are healthier.

Organic foods behave differently in cooking than the so-called conventional foods. You will not get good results if you try to substitute conventional ingredients for the organic ones. The difference between organic produce and non-organic produce is extreme. They are not the same product, and you cannot substitute one for the other.

Conventional vegetables are often loaded with pesticides and chemicals intended to prolong their shelf life, are almost always grown through the use of artificial fertilizers (made from petroleum), and have been designed for their appearance and shelf life. These characteristics have an impact on taste and nutrition. U.S. government agencies have stated that conventional fruits and vegetables are safe for human consumption.

Organic vegetables have been grown in good soil without the use of most pesticides and without artificial fertilizer, and are usually traditional varieties that were developed for taste and nutrition. They really do taste much better.

I am not saying that everything organic is good. There are some products that are just bad for people, even if they are organic. The best source of nutritional information is the Weston A. Price Foundation, which maintains an excellent website full of vital information about nutrition and health. I highly recommend that you visit their website at www.westonaprice.org.

Selecting Grassfed Meat

First, make sure the meat is grassfed and grass finished.

Just about every cow, bison, and lamb is fed grass at some point in its life. The meat we call grassfed is also grass finished, which means that it is not finished on grains and other feed.

The meat does not need to be certified organic to be grassfed. The animals should be fed living grass and meadow plants right in the pasture when the weather allows, and dried grass and forage in the winter. If they are fed anything else, they are not grassfed. (It's fine if calves and lambs get milk from their mothers.) The animals should not be given growth hormones, antibiotics, or any kind of growth promotant. The animals should not be fed any kind of grain, such as wheat, corn, barley, etc. They should never be given any kind of soyfeed. They should not be fed any kind of animal byproduct. The point is that the animals should be eating what they have been designed to eat: grass, meadow plants, and dried grass, and that's about it.

It should be understood that meat can be certified organic without being grassfed, and that most of the "organic" beef, bison, and lamb sold in the U.S. are fed soybeans, grains, and other substances that are not grass.

Selecting the Cut

It is important to become familiar with the different cuts of beef and what they can be used for. No matter how good the meat, you're not going to get a tender steak out of brisket, or a flavorful pot roast out of tenderloin.

In general, beef can be divided into three types of cuts: tender cuts; not so tender cuts; and those cuts which are in-between. It must be understood that all these cuts can be made tender, if the appropriate cooking method is used.

1. **Tender Cuts:** Delmonico, New York steak, Porterhouse, rib roast, ribeye, sirloin, strip loin, T-bone, and tenderloin. These cuts are great for roasting, grilling, sautéing, or broiling.

2. **In-Between Cuts:** cross rib, flank, hanger steak, shoulder, sirloin tip, skirt, tri-tip, and certain parts of the chuck, such as the flat iron. These cuts are good for roasting, grilling, sautéing, or broiling, though more care has to be taken with their preparation. They are also appropriate for pot roasting, braising, or stewing.

3. **Not So Tender Cuts:** arm roast, brisket, bottom round, most of the chuck, round, rump, and stew meat. These cuts are only suitable for pot roasting, braising, or stewing.

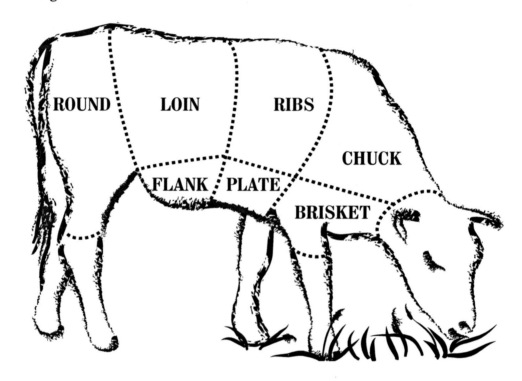

About Grassfed Fat

Grassfed beef is much leaner than factory beef. The best grassfed beef has some marbling. Marbling is the tiny flecks of white fat that you should be able to see in the meat. The more marbling, the more tender and tasty the beef. It should be noted that fat from grassfed beef is extremely healthy, as well as flavorful. A nice fat cap on a roast or steak adds great flavor, and really helps in cooking.

Grassfed bison does not have marbling. Neither does grassfed lamb. A fat cap for lamb and bison really helps, both for flavor and cooking.

Cooking Oil

Most of the cooking oils used today are a product of modern food technology. They were not eaten for most of history. They do not tenderize, or add good flavor to food. They have no place in this book. To learn more about modern oils, I suggest you visit www.westonaprice.org, the website of the Weston A. Price Foundation, which has a great deal of information on the subject.

I only use five traditional vegetable oils. Each of these oils has particular qualities, and has been chosen for a particular purpose in each recipe. It is very important that you use the exact oil called for in a recipe. Please do not substitute, except where indicated.

1. **Extra Virgin Olive Oil, Unfiltered and Organic** is the oil of choice for marinating meat. It lubricates and tenderizes meat without making it mushy. It carries other marinade flavors deep into the meat. The oil must be unfiltered, as filtering removes the very part of the oil (lipids and enzymes) that tenderizes the meat. It has no particular advantage over filtered oil when used for frying or sautéing, as heat destroys the enzymes. It is also great in salad dressings.

2. **Extra Virgin Olive Oil, Organic.** This oil is great for all cooking purposes, such as sautéing, browning, or frying. It will not tenderize meat, as the lipids and enzymes have been removed by filtering.

3. **Extra Virgin Coconut Oil, Organic.** This oil is very good for cooking purposes. It does have a strong flavor which is not to everyone's liking, and which can overwhelm the natural flavor of good meat. I like to use it in curries and other spicy dishes.

4. **Unrefined Sesame Oil, Organic.** This oil is good for all cooking purposes.

5. **Unrefined Toasted Sesame Oil, Organic.** This oil has a strong, nutty, aromatic flavor. It is often used to flavor Asian dishes. The flavor goes particularly well with beef. It is used for flavoring and marinating.

A number of traditionally made European olive oils are the equivalent of organic, and can be used.

Oils to Avoid

The wrong oil can ruin any dish. All modern vegetable oils should be avoided. The following non-traditional oils should never be used for these recipes.

Canola Oil

Corn Oil

Cottonseed Oil

Soybean Oil

It does not matter if some of these modern vegetable oils are organic, or cold pressed, or expeller pressed, they still should not be used.

Animal Fat

The very words "animal fat" are enough to make most people shudder, these words conjure up fears of all kinds of deadly diseases, fears that have been created by a huge and pervasive marketing campaign. The truth of the matter is that we need to eat fat to be healthy, and the very best fat you can eat is the right kind of animal fat and fish fat. Traditional peoples knew this and ate huge quantities of good animal fat. This is explained in detail at the website of the Weston A. Price Foundation.

Fat is essential for tender grassfed meat. The right kind of animal fat can give you wonderful results and wonderful flavor. It also works better in cooking than modern vegetable oils, artificial fats, and factory fats.

What is the right kind of animal fat? It must come from animals that have been naturally raised and fed, without the use of hormones, antibiotics, feed loaded with pesticides, and other unnatural ingredients.

If you eat fat, milk, and butter from animals that have been properly raised and fed, you will be nourishing your body with the high quality nutrients in the fat, milk, and butter from pastured, grassfed animals.

Butter

It is important to use only the right kind of butter. Most of the butters available have been made from factory milk. They are full of water, which causes them to spatter when cooking. Many of these butters are mixed with vegetable oils such as canola oil, and have various chemicals added to them.

The right kind of butter comes from organic milk. It should be pure butter, with no added oils, chemicals, or water. However, just being organic is not enough. The cows should be raised on pasture. Pastured butter tastes much better, is very healthy, and melts and cooks without spattering. I use only this type of butter, and the recipes will not work with any other kind. Many of the same farmers who sell grassfed beef also sell excellent pastured butter.

Pastured butter was what our ancestors used, and there is no substitute.

Beef Fat

Beef fat is one of the tastiest and most nutritious fats you can use, as long as it comes from grassfed cattle.

The best place for beef fat to be is right on the meat as you cook it. A one-quarter inch fat cap will do wonders for flavor and tenderness. (Thicker is better.) It will also provide superb flavor to any vegetables roasting along with the meat, such as potatoes and carrots. Unfortunately, most producers super-trim their meat, slicing off the very fat that provides flavor and tenderness. Replacing this fat is necessary for so many recipes. The best replacement for beef fat is — beef fat. Fortunately, many producers sell this in the form of suet and beef lard, also known as beef tallow.

Beef Suet is composed of little pieces of fat. This is usually sold in large containers, but you can freeze what you do not use, and thaw as necessary.

Beef Tallow is beef fat and/or beef suet which has been melted and strained. In its solid form, it is hard and brittle. My refrigerator always has a jar of beef tallow.

Whether suet or tallow, beef fat has many uses, including: replacing a trimmed off fat cap, basting, roasting, frying, and sautéing. It withstands high temperatures well without breaking down. Grassfed beef fat is also a nutritional powerhouse, being full of omega-3 fatty acids and CLA.

Finally, you can substitute beef tallow for butter in any recipe that calls for butter.

Lamb Fat

Grassfed lamb fat is sold in the form of suet or lamb tallow. It is less versatile than beef fat or pork lard, but can provide wonderful flavor when properly used. Lamb fat is excellent for replacing a trimmed off fat cap, and for basting. It is at its best when used to lubricate roast vegetables, especially potatoes.

Lamb fat can have an unpleasant, greasy texture when it congeals, so food cooked with lamb fat should be served hot. Lamb fat has a low smoking point, and can smell bad when it gets too hot. Lamb fat should be used for frying only at low to medium temperatures.

Lard

Lard was once the most common cooking fat in America. (It is still the most popular cooking fat in much of the world, including China.) The reputation of lard was destroyed by a clever marketing campaign. Most people switched to hydrogenated oils and vegetable oils. It is now almost impossible to find natural, unhydrogenated lard in any grocery store.

Hydrogenated lard (which is usually all that is available) should never be used in cooking because it has had its very structure chemically altered — which ruins its taste. It does have a great shelf life though.

Lard should come from naturally raised pigs, and must be unhydrogenated. The best source I have found is Dietrich's Meats, in Krumsville, Pennsylvania. Their lard is so outstanding it is like a work of art, or a fine wine. Fortunately, they do ship this superb product. Lard is excellent for frying, sautéing, stir-frying, providing fat to meats, adding flavor, and baking. It has a soft, spreadable consistency that makes it easy to work with. It behaves well in the pan, and can withstand high temperatures without breaking down.

Bacon

Bacon is used in several recipes in this book for its fat and flavor. It is worth going to the website of the bacon producer to make sure that their pigs have been traditionally raised on natural feed.

It is also important to be sure that the bacon is free of preservatives (other than salt), and artificial ingredients.

Lean bacon is an absurdity. The only purpose of using bacon is for its fat, which aids in cooking and provides great flavor. Be sure to inspect each package carefully to make sure that the bacon strips are mostly fat. Lean bacon just won't work in these recipes.

If you do not want to use bacon, you can substitute butter or beef tallow.

Salt

The kind of salt you use will have a dramatic effect on your cooking, not to mention your health.

There are those who say all salt is sea salt, and that there is no difference. While it is true that all salt originated at some time from the sea, there is a tremendous difference in how it is processed, and what else is included in the salt. This makes a huge difference in taste, and how the salt affects the food.

Refined salt is bleached with chemicals, and has had just about all of the minerals that are in natural salt removed. This results in a product so bitter that they add sugar or some other sweetener to make it palatable. Manufacturers of refined salt often add other ingredients, such as aluminum products and artificial iodine. The effect of these refined salts on the cooking process, not to mention taste, is terrible.

Unrefined salt that has been harvested by traditional methods retains the natural minerals, lacks artificial additives, has a better effect on food, and just tastes better. There are many varieties.

Since they are gathered in different parts of the world, and naturally include various minerals and other substances, there can be a dramatic variation in taste. There can be quite a difference in color. Some salts are grey, some are different shades of white, one is even red. The two types of salt I use are:

1. **RealSalt®.** This salt is mined from an ancient seabed in Utah. It comes in two sizes: fine and Kosher. It is white in color, but with many different colored flecks. This salt contains trace minerals. This salt behaves superbly in cooking and has a wonderful flavor.

2. **Unrefined Sea Salt.** This salt is moist, grey in color, contains trace minerals, and has a wonderful flavor. It has large crystals, which I usually crush with a rolling pin when seasoning meat, so that the salt is more evenly distributed and absorbed. Celtic Sea Salt® is an excellent brand.

I have used other unrefined sea salts, some from Hawaii and Portugal, but the above is what I usually use. These salts are considerably more expensive than factory salt, but the difference in taste, health, and cooking qualities are worth it. If you substitute an inferior salt, you will have inferior results.

Spices and Condiments

Grassfed meat has a wonderful flavor, when properly cooked. Most of the recipes in this book try to bring out that flavor, rather than mask it with spices and condiments. Even one or two ingredients can be very important to the taste of the dish. It is crucial to have good ingredients, as inferior ones will ruin the taste of any dish.

This means, as a minimum, that all herbs, spices, and condiments must be organic, or the equivalent. But just being labeled organic is not enough. Many organic products are full of undesirable ingredients, such as soy products and canola oil.

Non-organic spices are very often irradiated for greater shelf life. The manufacturers add all kinds of chemicals as preservatives and flavor enhancers. Most condiments include some form of MSG, some soy product, and high fructose corn syrup. I would not use anything with any of those ingredients.

Organic herbs and spices have much more flavor.

Fresh Herbs

These should, without exception, be organic, or the equivalent. It is best to have these locally grown, as they do not travel well. Italian parsley, sage, rosemary, and thyme are the ones I use most often, though I also use oregano, marjoram, cilantro, and basil.

Dried Herbs

Good quality dried herbs can add wonderful flavor. These must be organic, or the equivalent. The best dried herbs I have ever used are grown wild in Sardinia. They are marketed by A.G. Ferrari. While they are very expensive compared to other organic brands, their flavor and aroma are without parallel. The dried herbs I use most often are thyme, oregano, marjoram, and sage.

Spices

It is vitally important to only buy organic spices because the flavor is so much better. I also use some spices from different areas of Europe, such as Spain and Portugal, which, while not labeled organic, have been produced by traditional methods, and grown in good soil.

Spice Blends

Again, these should be organic, but you have to be very careful because so many spice blends labeled organic contain some kind of soy product or modern vegetable oil, such as canola oil. I usually make my own spice blends out of organic ingredients.

Vegetables, Herbs, and Fruits

Fresh vegetables and fresh herbs can really improve the flavor and even the tenderness of grassfed meats. They are crucial in pot roasts and stews for giving body, texture, and flavor to the gravy. If organic, or the equivalent, they can be very nutritious. They can be the key components of great side dishes. But the vegetables must be of the highest quality.

In other words, great vegetables can improve almost any dish, mediocre vegetables will result in a mediocre dish, and poor vegetables will ruin almost any dish.

Unfortunately, most of the vegetables available in the U.S. are poor in quality. This is because most of them have been modified for purposes that have nothing to do with nutrition or taste.

Why Factory Produce is Modified

Factory produce is modified for three reasons: to increase shelf life, to increase tolerance of pesticides, and for appearance.

1. **Shelf Life** means the amount of time the vegetable can sit on the supermarket shelves without appearing spoiled.

2. **Tolerance of Pesticides** means that the plant can absorb more pesticides before dying. This means that you ingest more pesticides when you eat the vegetable. Many of these pesticides penetrate deeply into the plant, and cannot be removed by washing. Some vegetables have been genetically modified to have an internal pesticide that cannot be removed from the plant.

3. **Appearance** means that the vegetable or fruit looks much better than it tastes.

All of these unnatural modifications increase profits, but do nothing for taste or nutrition.

Another problem is that most conventional vegetables and fruits have been grown in soil that has been depleted of almost all minerals and nutrients through the use of artificial fertilizer. These products have very little nutrition, and even less taste.

Organic Vegetables, Herbs, and Fruits Taste Better

I value nutrition and taste above all else. I want to eat food that is as fresh as possible. When food looks good, I want it to taste as good as it looks. This means that all the vegetables, herbs, and fruits I use are organic, or the equivalent. All the recipes in this book have been made only with vegetables, herbs, and fruits that are organic, or the equivalent.

Organic vegetables, herbs, and fruits are supposed to be grown in good natural soil, without the use of artificial fertilizers or pesticides. Usually, they are traditional varieties that were developed for taste. True organic food tastes so much better.

Note that I said supposed to. Just because something is labeled "organic" does not always mean that it is of high quality. The growing popularity of organic produce has led some of the giant factory farm agribusinesses to produce their own "organic" products. The issue has been raised as to whether these products are actually organic. The government has shown no interest in enforcing organic standards on the big companies, even where documented complaints have been made. This means you have to pay careful attention to the quality of what you buy. If it tastes like factory food, it probably IS factory food, no matter what the label says.

Buy Local

It is best if you can buy from a local farmer who raises organic produce, or from a grocer who sells produce from local farmers. Curiously enough, the government inspects small farmers rigorously and enforces all rules, regulations, and standards upon them. This means that organic produce from small producers is almost certain to actually be organic.

I ask you to join me, and many others, in supporting small farmers and small producers. We'll all eat better, tastier, and healthier if we do.

Another huge problem is the large number of "organic" products from other countries. Some of these countries use pesticides and other chemicals that are so toxic that they have been banned even in the United States. I have found organic produce, olive oil, and spices from Argentina and Canada to be excellent. I think that products from Europe labeled organic probably are organic, due to the standards there. Many grocers will not label the country of origin for their produce. If they don't label it, I don't buy it.

Organic Food Under Attack

The media has reported several studies that claim that organic food is no more nutritious than "conventional" (factory) food, and that organic food is less safe than the "conventional" variety. I just don't believe these studies. They are in total conflict with my own experience, and that of my friends and family. They are contradicted by other studies. It is always important in evaluating the objectivity of studies, to pay careful attention to who funded the study, and to the motivations of those conducting the study.

I believe organic food is more nutritious and tastes much better. More people than ever before are starting to realize this.

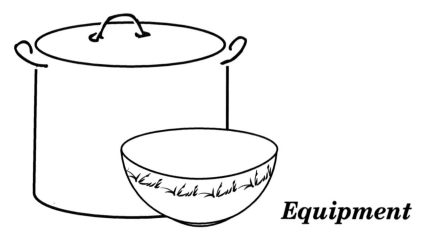

Equipment

Pans and Cookware

The pans and cookware you use can have a dramatic effect on the success of your cooking and the taste of your food. The cookware can also have a powerful effect on your health.

Good cookware should not discolor or change the taste of your food. It should conduct heat well. It should not release poison into your food, or give off toxic fumes. If the cookware is well greased, food should not stick to it.

The cookware I use meets all of these conditions. I use cast iron, enameled cookware, and stainless steel.

Cast Iron

Cast iron is my first preference for steaks and every kind of sautéing, pan broiling, and frying, as well as for stews and pot roasts. Well-seasoned cast iron cookware is non-stick, (if you do not cook at really high temperatures, which I never do). Cast iron cookware's heat retention qualities and weight make it the best possible choice for steaks, though you could use a heavy bottomed stainless steel frying pan. Cast iron is also relatively inexpensive, and will last forever with simple care. The more you cook with it, the better it gets. If well-seasoned, it is easy to clean, though you cannot put it in a dishwasher.

Cast iron will rust, if you don't take care of it. The care required is easy. As the pan becomes more seasoned, the care required is even easier.

Cast iron pans must be seasoned to work well. Many cast iron pans are sold in a pre-seasoned state. I prefer to buy the traditional, unseasoned cast iron, and to season it myself.

Enameled Cookware

Enameled cookware is nonreactive. Food usually does not stick to it if the pan is well greased, and the heat is not too high. I use enameled roasting pans all the time. Stews and pot roasts also work very well in enameled pans. However, I find that cast iron works much better than enamel for sautéing, pan broiling, and frying.

Stainless Steel Cookware

I use stainless steel for many cooking purposes. Stainless steel is supposed to be nonreactive. However, concerns have recently been raised that some stainless steel pots and pans are reactive and leach heavy metals, such as nickel, into the food. I have not noticed any such problems with my stainless steel cookware, which I have had for many years. While these pans are not non-stick, a good coating of high quality fat, like butter or olive oil, will prevent or reduce sticking.

Other Cookware

It should be understood that all the recipes in this book have been tested with the cookware that I use, and substituting other cookware may not work well. If you do not want to use cast iron, you could get acceptable results by using stainless steel and/or enameled cookware for everything, providing that any frying pan or casserole has a thick, heavy bottom.

I never use any cookware with aluminum in it. The aluminum can leach right into your food, ruining its taste, color, and more importantly, your health. Aluminum has been linked to Alzheimer's and other diseases, and I do not want it in my body. This also means that I do not let aluminum foil touch any food. Since many people are now wary of aluminum cookware, manufacturers give names to their cookware that do not mention aluminum, but the aluminum is often there, in one form or another.

I never use any kind of cookware that is advertised as "non-stick," because they always contain new materials that were never used in traditional cooking. I don't want these substances, which were originally developed for use in aircraft or spaceships, in my body.

Traditional cookware, like traditional food, is best.

Seasoning a Cast Iron Pan

1. Clean the new pan with good natural soap and hot water, using a steel wool pad or a good stiff brush. The object is to remove any shipping coating and/ or metal dust from the pan. Rinse well, and dry completely. Coat the pan all over with olive oil, covering every surface inside and out.

2. Cover the lowest rack of your oven with foil, so it will catch any dripping grease.

3. Put the pan on the top rack of the oven. Turn the temperature to bake at 350 degrees, and close the door. When the temperature reaches 350 degrees, bake for 2 hours. Turn the heat off, and let the pan cool completely in the closed oven. I usually plan this so that the pan can cool down in the oven overnight.

4. Remove the pan from the oven, and wipe off with paper towels to remove any excess oil. You are now ready to cook!

5. Every time you cook, the pan will get more seasoned. Clean with hot water and a stiff brush after use. Salt works very well at removing dirt that resists the water and the brush. Dry after cleaning, and coat very lightly with olive oil. Your pan will soon develop that beautiful black surface that is smooth, shiny, and non-stick. It will get better every time you use it.

Bags and Containers

We have to use some kind of container or bag to marinate, or to store food in the refrigerator. Traditionally, this was done in ceramic or glass bowls, or in cloth bags. More recently, plastic containers and plastic bags, and the ever-present aluminum foil, have been widely used.

I do not let aluminum foil touch anything that will be eaten, because I do not want the aluminum in my body.

Many plastics used for food storage contain or consist of PVC (polyvinyl chloride), whose safety for food storage has been questioned. Other types of plastic used for food storage are considered safe. Whether or not they are safe, I have at times experienced an off-taste when I have marinated meat in plastic bags or containers. The off-taste could only have come from some part of the plastic leaching into and/or interacting with the marinade.

I prefer to use glass and ceramic containers, which do not release foreign substances into the food, and are reusable.

Ovens and Ranges

The recipes in this book were prepared on a conventional electric range and in a conventional electric oven. A conventional gas range and gas oven should also work. If you have a wood burning stove or oven, and are good at controlling the temperature, these recipes should work fine.

Microwave ovens will not work with these recipes. Failure is guaranteed. Microwave ovens cook from the inside out, and the cooking process is totally different.

These recipes have not been tested in a convection oven. A convection oven cooks differently than a conventional oven, and I doubt the recipes would work. I used to own a convection oven, and found that grain fed beef came out tougher and less tasty than the same beef cooked in a conventional oven.

These recipes have not been tested on a glass top stove. You should check the manufacturers' instructions before you try using a heavy pan on such a stove.

These recipes work so well on a conventional range and a conventional oven that there is no need to use anything else.

Cutting Boards

The kind of cutting board you use is also important. The only good choice is a wooden cutting board. This has been the overwhelming choice of humankind for most of history. Recently, the market has been deluged with various plastic "boards." The plastic "boards" should never be used.

Why not plastic? You will, without doubt, cut into the plastic while cutting and chopping food. This will release the chemicals in the plastic into your food. Not only could these chemicals be harmful to your health, they can and will adversely affect the taste, and sometimes even the color of your food. They can interfere with the cooking process as well.

Research has discovered that wooden cutting boards have natural substances within the wood that inhibit the growth of bacteria. Most bacteria will not survive on a dry wooden board. Plastic does not have these natural antibacterial substances.

Just use wood.

Techniques for Tender Grassfed Meat

Salting Techniques

To salt or not to salt, that is the question. After much cooking, with and without salt, I have come to the conclusion that (with the definite exception of bison) all meat benefits from the addition of good natural sea salt.

Another question of equal importance is when to salt.

The experts have been divided on this issue for years. Some adamantly insist that you should never salt meat before cooking. They claim that pre-salting causes the meat to lose juices, making it tougher. They also claim that it brings moisture to the surface of the meat, making it impossible to seal properly. Other experts just as adamantly insist that meat should be salted long before cooking, claiming that this improves the flavor of the meat by giving the salt time to penetrate, and concentrates the flavor of the meat by drawing out excess liquid.

Again, after much cooking, I've come to the conclusion that both sides are right. The difference is in the meat itself.

Grassfed beef has much less water than factory beef, and much more flavor. Salting grassfed beef too much in advance will toughen the meat, draw out juices, and make the surface wet and sticky. The salt will also overwhelm the natural flavor of the meat.

Pre-salting factory beef will draw out some of the excess water. It will not toughen factory beef, which is saturated with water. Because of the water, the surface of factory beef is always wet anyway. Factory beef has very little flavor to begin with, and that little bit is of such poor quality that it should be overwhelmed by pre-salting, or by strong marinades and sauces.

When to Salt Grassfed Meat?

We are cooking grassfed meat in this book. Grassfed beef should be salted before cooking, but only just before cooking, and only lightly. This kind of salting does not toughen the meat or make it wet, and helps bring out the superb natural flavor.

Grassfed bison should never be salted before cooking. The early explorers noted that the Native Americans did not salt bison, and also remarked that the bison did not need it. They were right. Pre-salting bison makes it tougher, and overwhelms the sweet, natural flavor.

Grassfed lamb can be pre-salted without any adverse results. This type of salting is best done as part of a rub or marinade, and can greatly improve the flavor of the meat.

What Kind of Salt?

I only use natural, unrefined sea salt. Sea salt usually comes in a coarse grind. I usually crush the salt with a rolling pin before I use it. This seems to give the best results, as it makes the salt easier to spread evenly, and avoids the problem of biting into some big crystals of salt.

Natural, unrefined sea salt tastes much better and brings out the natural flavor of grassfed meat.

Temperature of the Meat

For steaks and roasts, I consider grassfed beef and grassfed bison to be done when the meat thermometer shows a temperature of 115 to 130 degrees, which gives you meat ranging from rare to medium rare. Lamb can be tasty and palatable up to the 140 to 150 degree range.

This book contains a large number of steaks and roasts, all intended to be rare to medium rare. After much study, I consider this degree of doneness to provide the most nutrients. After much tasting, I consider this degree of doneness to be absolutely delicious.

Safe Room Temperature and Meat Safety

Many of the recipes in this book call for marinating at room temperature, and all but one call for letting the meat come to room temperature before cooking.

Room temperature means that the meat is cool to the touch, not cold, not warm. The times given for marinating and bringing meat to room temperature are the times I use. These times are based on the temperatures in my kitchen. You should use these times as a guide, and modify them based on the temperature in your kitchen.

Food safety is a hot issue these days, and the authorities have issued a number of rules and guidelines. Those guidelines were developed for factory meat.

I give you no advice at all regarding food safety, and I will not repeat the guidelines here.

I have eaten the recipes in this book over a thousand times. I have always felt renewed and invigorated after eating. This has been true not only for me, but for my family, and everyone else who I have cooked for.

The choice, and the risk (to the extent there is any), is yours.

What If There Is No Fat Cap?

"Living off the fat of the land" used to mean wealth, luxury, success, and great eating. Unfortunately, we live in a time when the irrational fear of saturated animal fat has greatly reduced the quality of food. This fat phobia has resulted in almost every meat packer in the country trimming almost every vestige of exterior fat on almost every cut of meat. Since a good fat cap is absolutely necessary for many fine dishes, this fat phobia is a culinary disaster. Since fat from grassfed animals is one of the most nutritious foods available, this is also a nutritional disaster.

A fat cap on a roast is a layer of fat that covers the top of the meat. The fat cap bastes the meat as it roasts, preventing it from drying out, and provides wonderful flavor to the meat. A fat cap on a steak is a layer of fat that covers one edge of the steak. Even one-quarter inch of fat will do, though more would be better. This helps immeasurably in many kinds of recipes. You don't have to actually eat the fat cap, though I do. The crisp brown fat on a roast or steak is delicious, as well as nutritious.

Natural saturated fats from grassfed animals are healthy. The best place to learn about fat is the website of the Weston A. Price Foundation (www.westonaprice.org). I suggest the article "The Skinny on Fats."

Good animal fat provides great benefits of taste and tenderness when used properly.

Substitutes for a Fat Cap

You can help a roast that lacks a fat cap. If your roast does not have a fat cap, or if your fat cap covers only part of the roast, you can fix the situation by covering the top of the roast with any of the following:

- Thinly sliced pastured butter

- Thin slices or shavings of beef tallow

- Pieces of beef suet

- Natural, unhydrogenated lard

- Slices of fat, traditionally made bacon

- Slices of fat, traditionally made beef bacon

- There is one other method you can use to provide a substitute fat cap. For reasons that I have never understood, it is common to find some fat on the bottom, or sides, or ends of the roast, where it will do absolutely no good, while the top has been scraped clean of all fat. In this case, I will trim the fat from the useless areas and place it on top of the roast. These pieces often fall off during the roasting process, but cutting grooves into them helps them stay on top.

Finally, lobby your grassfed meat producer to leave a fat cap on top of their meat. If enough of us do this, it could happen.

Roasting Grassfed Meat

Roasting is one of the best ways to create tender and flavorful grassfed meat. Done right, it creates a nicely browned exterior, delicious with concentrated flavor, and a tender, juicy, flavorful interior. While roasting is a simple process, there are some rules that should be followed to achieve tenderness and flavor. Once you are familiar with these rules, they will become automatic.

Rule 1.   **Marinate or pre-brown the meat.**

Because grassfed beef and bison are so lean, they need some help to reach the peak of flavor and tenderness. I have found three techniques that work well: marinating the meat in unfiltered olive oil; marinating the meat in a mixture based on crushed vegetables; and pre-browning the meat. Any of these three techniques, done in advance, will make the roast much more tender and flavorful.

Rule 2.   **Use unfiltered, organic, extra virgin olive oil for marinating.**

Since this oil is unfiltered, it still has its natural enzymes, which really penetrate and tenderize the meat. Filtered olive oil lacks these enzymes, and is much less effective.

Rule 3.   **Never use any kind of wine, vinegar, or salt in a marinade for beef or bison.**

They will toughen the meat.

Rule 4.   **Always bring the roast to room temperature before you roast it.**

Room temperature means that the roast is cool to the touch, not cold. Putting cold meat in a hot oven will make it tough.

Rule 5.   **Always place the roasting pan on the next to lowest oven rack position.**

All the recipes were tested with this position. The oven position does matter.

Rule 6.   **Use the High-Low Method.**

The traditional method of roasting meat was to start with a hot fire, which cooled as the roasting progressed. The initial heat sealed the meat and gave it a tasty crust, while the falling temperature resulted in a tender, delicious roast. Most of the roast recipes honor this tradition by starting with a relatively high heat, and finishing with a much lower heat. When the heat is lowered in the oven, the temperature gradually decreases, which reproduces the effect of a cooling fire.

Rule 7.   **Baste with the pan drippings.**

This really helps keep the meat tender and flavorful. Most of the recipes call for only one or two bastings, usually just before the heat is reduced. Even one basting makes a huge difference.

Rule 8.   **Slice the roast against the grain of the meat.**

This also helps make the roast more tender.

Follow these rules and you will be rewarded with tender grassfed meat that is absolutely delicious.

Twice Cooking Grassfed Meat, No Marinade Needed

This is another excellent technique for creating tender grassfed meat. No marinade is needed. The meat is literally cooked twice. First, it is browned, then it rests, then it is cooked a second time. While resting, something happens to the meat that makes it infinitely more tender and flavorful.

You need a sizeable piece of meat (at least two pounds). You can cut the large piece of meat into smaller steaks after the resting period, and finish them individually.

There are two ways to do the browning. The one I use most often is to sauté the meat in butter or other good fat. However, you can also brown it in the oven without using any fat.

Pan Browning

1. Make sure the meat is at room temperature. It should be at least 2 pounds.

2. Melt 2 tablespoons of pastured butter in a heavy bottomed frying pan, over medium heat.

3. When the butter is hot and slightly smoking, brown the meat evenly on all sides, turning as necessary to avoid scorching. When the meat is browned on all sides, put it on a plate, and let it cool. When the meat is cool, refrigerate overnight, or let it rest an additional hour or two at room temperature.

4. Finish cooking the meat. The individual recipes give instructions on how to do this. If you are not using a recipe, the main thing to remember is that the pre-browned meat will cook much faster, taking about half to two-thirds the time of marinated meat. The size and thickness of the piece of meat are important factors in how long it will take to finish the meat.

Oven Browning

1. Make sure the meat is at room temperature. It should be at least 2 pounds.

2. Preheat the oven to 425 degrees.

3. Place the roast on a well-greased roasting pan. Roast in the oven for 10 to 15 minutes, or until the roast is browned on all sides.

4. When the meat is browned on all sides, put it on a plate, and let it cool. When the meat is cool, refrigerate overnight, or let it rest an additional hour or two at room temperature.

5. Finish cooking the meat. The individual recipes give instructions on how to do this. If you are not using a recipe, the main thing to remember is that the pre-browned meat will cook much faster, taking about half to two-thirds the time of marinated meat. The size and thickness of the piece of meat are important factors in how long it will take to finish the meat.

Freezer Aging, an Easy Method for Tender Grassfed Meat

I came across this method both by research and accident. I learned in my research that Siberians would often wrap fresh meat in a package, dig a hole in the frozen ground, bury the package, and eat the meat several weeks to several months later. This was supposed to result in really tender meat. I also learned that hunters will often put wild game in the freezer for a couple of months before eating, claiming that this made the meat much more tender. Both of these methods seemed to take too long, and I was not convinced that they would work.

I learned differently when I thawed a roast that I had kept in my freezer for about six weeks, and cooked it. The roast was considerably more tender and flavorful than a similar roast which had not been aged in the freezer. I remembered my earlier research, and decided to experiment. What I finally learned was that keeping meat in the freezer in the original wrapper for a few weeks to a couple of months, will result in meat that is somewhat more tender. However, I found a better way to wrap the meat that resulted in a much more tender roast.

How to Wrap Grassfed Meat for Freezer Aging

1. Remove the wrapper from the meat.

2. Brush all surfaces of the meat with extra virgin olive oil. In this case, the oil does not have to be unfiltered.

3. Wrap the meat in natural wax paper.

4. Place the wrapped meat in a heavy duty plastic freezer bag, squeezing out as much air as possible before sealing the bag.

5. Freeze the meat for 3 weeks to 3 months. Thaw and cook in the usual manner.

Pot Roasting Grassfed Meat

Pot roasting is a technique that can make tougher cuts exquisitely tender and delicious. It has been a traditional favorite in Europe and the United States, and some wonderful flavor combinations have been developed. Though some authorities maintain that you can use conventional recipes for pot roasting grassfed beef, I disagree in part. You can use a recipe designed for conventional meat, but the results will be mediocre and only moderately tender. I have customized my pot roasting techniques to suit grassfed meat, and the results have been spectacular, both in taste and tenderness. The differences are crucial.

1. **Marinade.** For grassfed meat in a pot roast, the marinade should either have no salt, or very little salt. Pre-salting grassfed meat seems to toughen it. The marinade should not contain wine or vinegar. While it is traditional to use wine and vinegar to marinate meat, these substances will make grassfed meat tough. I believe the original reason for using wine and vinegar in marinades was to preserve the meat, not tenderize it.

2. **Pre-Browning.** Grassfed meat should be pre-browned as part of making the pot roast. This pre-browning is a crucial step, and must be done properly. This means that the surface of the meat should be dry, the meat should not have been pre-salted, and there should be plenty of good fat in the pan. This means butter, olive oil, beef tallow, bacon fat, pork lard, or lamb tallow. The heat should never rise above medium. The meat must be turned evenly to make sure that all sides are brown, without being scorched. Once the roast is browned, it should rest for a while before the next cooking step. I usually brown the roast, put it to rest, and let it sit while I peel and chop the vegetables, and arrange the other ingredients. You could brown the roast the night before you plan to cook it. The combination of pre-browning and resting really tenderizes the meat.

3. **Cookware.** It is important to use the right kind of cookware. I always use a well-seasoned cast iron casserole with a cast iron lid. Enameled cast iron would also work. A thick, heavy pot is needed for pot roasting. The roast should not be much smaller than the pot, and the pot should be pretty full, once all the meat, vegetables and liquid are inside.

4. **Broth.** It is essential to use a good, natural, traditional broth, such as ***Nomad's Broth, Beef Broth, Bison Broth***, or ***Chicken Broth***, (see pages 45 - 53). These broths, which must be homemade, are loaded with flavor and nutrients that help keep the meat tender while adding a wonderful flavor to the dish.

5. **Simmering.** When the meat is simmering, the liquid should be bubbling slowly. Many cooking authorities have stated that the liquid should just barely bubble, but I get better results with a slow, but consistent bubble.

6. **Testing for Doneness.** Grassfed meat cooks faster, and your pot roast could be done a lot sooner than you would expect. When the skewer or fork goes in easily, it is ready.

7. **Gravy.** The vegetables should cook together with meat from the beginning to the end of the simmering process. This means that some of the vegetables will break up, disintegrate and become mushy, but they will fully release their flavor and goodness into the dish. This is the way it was done traditionally, and makes the most delicious pot roast.

Stir-Frying Grassfed Meat

Traditionally, stir-frying is done at very high heat. However, the countries that invented this tradition rarely stir-fried beef. While stir-frying at very high temperatures works for factory and grain finished beef, grassfed is different.

I have found that stir-frying grassfed beef should be done only at medium high heat. The cooking time should also be very brief. The meat should be stir-fried for no longer than it takes for all parts of the pieces to lose their pink color. This will usually happen in 1 to 2 minutes. The meat should be stirred regularly while cooking. Any vegetables should be stir-fried separately, and added to the meat as soon as the meat is ready, then mixed thoroughly.

Stir-frying is not recommended for grassfed bison.

Grassfed lamb can be stir-fried at high heat, or at medium high heat.

No Need for Soy, Just Try Fish Sauce

We decided to eliminate all soy from our diet after researching soy foods. Once again, the website of the Weston A. Price Foundation provided valuable information. This led to a cooking problem — we really enjoyed various types of Asian dishes. Just about every one of them had some soy sauce.

The solution to the problem came from researching Thai and Vietnamese dishes. Fish sauce was used as a flavoring.

Fish sauce is made from the whole bodies (including all organs) of many small fish. Salt is added. When the process is complete, fish sauce in its final form is a fermented, clear liquid that is loaded with vital nutrients. While most people think of it only in connection with Thai, Vietnamese, and Filipino cooking, fish sauce has a long history that goes back to ancient Greece and Rome. The ancient Greeks called it garos, and used it to flavor all kinds of dishes. The Romans called it garum, and used it in almost every meat, fish, and fowl dish they cooked, instead of salt. There were many different kinds of garum, made from different kinds of fish, often with other ingredients added, such as a kind of grape concentrate. The Romans were the gourmets of the ancient world, and they knew flavor.

Fish sauce really enhances the flavor of the dish, and does not make it fishy. Just try **Grassfed Steak Kew** (see page 123). I now use fish sauce as a substitute for soy sauce. While the flavor is different, the taste is superb.

Part 2:
Recipes for
Tender Grassfed Meat

About the Recipes

Why Are the Recipes So Detailed?

These recipes provide detailed instructions on how to prepare them, so that even an inexperienced cook can make tender grassfed meat. The steps are quite simple, and once you get used to them, they will go very quickly and simply.

Most of the older cookbooks that I studied confined their actual cooking instructions to three words, "Cook until done." It was just assumed that people knew how to cook, which is not the case in our modern world. When I began cooking, I made a lot of mistakes, and ruined a number of dishes. Hopefully, these detailed instructions will help avoid those mistakes.

The other reason for the detail is that grassfed meat must be cooked differently. I was an experienced cook when I first started cooking grassfed meat. I learned the hard way that knowing how to cook factory meat is useless when cooking grassfed meat. These detailed instructions, if followed, will give you tender, delicious, grassfed meat.

Why Do So Many Recipes Have So Few Ingredients?

You will notice that many of the recipes seem to use the same ingredients. You will also notice that many of the recipes have only a few ingredients. This does not mean that every recipe is the same. In cooking, every detail is important and even a small variation can have a dramatic effect on the taste and success of a recipe.

One of the goals of this book is to give you recipes that will result in tender grassfed meat that is absolutely delicious. When properly cooked, grassfed beef and bison have a wonderful, deep, rich flavor that should not be masked by spices or sauces. This flavor can best be compared to that of a fine wine and it is my goal to bring out this flavor, rather than hide it. Once you have tasted how good this meat can be, you will not want to hide this taste with spices and sauces.

This is especially true of grassfed beef and grassfed bison. Grassfed lamb is often improved by additional flavors, and I use a lot more ingredients in those recipes.

Each cut of meat has its own characteristics, and the recipes are designed to take these differences into account. Some of the recipes for similar cuts of meat appear to be similar to each other. They are similar, not identical.

Why Do I Use High Heat in Roasting Grassfed Meat?

Most producers of grassfed beef and bison will advise you to use medium or low heat in cooking their meat. It is true that if you cook grassfed beef or bison at high heat from beginning to end, you will often end up with a tough piece of meat. But I have found that cooking with high heat at the beginning can add great flavor, and can result in a piece of meat that is even more tender than meat which is roasted at low to medium heat for the entire time.

I developed the High-Low Method by researching traditional ways of roasting meat. The only meat traditional people had was grassfed meat. My research revealed that the traditional method of roasting meat almost always began at a fairly high heat, which would be reduced consistently throughout the cooking time. This happened naturally as the fire burned down. This technique can be approximated in modern ovens by reducing the heat at specific intervals. Through trial and error, I have come up with cooking times that work very well, and will give you a more tender and flavorful piece of meat.

Broth

Beef Broth

About Broths

Some of the recipes call for broth as an ingredient. The broth not only adds liquid and flavor, but certain qualities that will help concentrate flavor and bind the taste of the dish together.

Only the right kind of broth will do. This is because a properly made broth will have many substances from the bones and cartilage that were used to prepare it, as well as many minerals and nutrients. All of these factors are completely missing from an improperly made broth.

What this means is that only homemade broth will do, and only homemade broth that is prepared properly. All ready-made broths, whether canned, bottled, or in cartons, (with very few exceptions[1]), are completely useless for our purposes. This is true even of the organic broths. Do not even think about using those cubes and powders. No ready-made broth has been properly cooked, and no ready-made broth contains the ingredients of a properly made homemade broth.

One of the major reasons that only a properly made homemade broth will do, is that no commercial broth is simmered long enough to get the proper nutrients, gelatin and other necessary substances out of the bones and cartilage. It takes at least 12 hours of simmering for these substances to leave the bones and become part of the broth.

The taste and cooking qualities of a good homemade broth are so wonderful and so much better than the factory broths.

I include recipes for **Beef Broth, Bison Broth, Lamb Broth, Chicken Broth, Turkey Broth, Nomad's Broth,** and **Quadruple Healing Broth.** Any of these broths can be used in the recipes. I am very grateful to Sally Fallon of the Weston A. Price Foundation for the wonderful knowledge of broth that she has provided. All of these recipes are based, at least in part, on the knowledge and techniques she provided in her cookbook, *Nourishing Traditions.*

In addition to being a superb cooking ingredient, these broths are loaded with minerals, natural gelatin, and other nutrients that make them extremely healthy and nourishing. I and my family have some broth twice a day. Our health has improved dramatically, in every respect, from this practice.

---

1   U.S. Wellness makes an excellent, healthy broth from grassfed marrow bones and other natural ingredients. (See **Sources**, page 217).

Simple Steps to Broth

Making broth may seem like a big project, especially if you have not done it before, but it is really very simple.

1. Put a bunch of ingredients (meat, bones, meat trimmings, assorted vegetables, and some salt) in a large stainless steel stockpot. Cover the ingredients with filtered water and a small amount of vinegar.

2. Heat the contents to boiling, skim off the scum, cover the pot, and let simmer for at least 12 hours.

3. Strain the broth into glass jars, and refrigerate so the fat rises to the top.

Broth Cooking Tips

1. Use only filtered water. Unfiltered water is full of chemicals, such as chlorine and fluoride, that will ruin the taste of your broth.

2. Always add the specified amount of organic unfiltered apple cider vinegar to your broth one-half hour to one hour before you start heating it. The vinegar will help the bones and cartilage release their nutrients into the broth.

3. Use only bones, meat, and trimmings from grassfed animals, or free range poultry. They are much more nutritious, and will give a much better flavor to your broth.

4. Use only organic (or the equivalent) vegetables. Non-organic vegetables are often full of pesticides, which will go right into your broth, ruining the taste. Organic vegetables are much more nutritious, and taste so much better.

5. Use only good, natural, unrefined sea salt. Factory salts have been stripped of their minerals, and often have other ingredients added to them, such as sugar and aluminum, which have no place in your broth. Natural, unrefined sea salt will add natural minerals to your broth, and tastes so much better. Two excellent brands are RealSalt® and Celtic Sea Salt®.

6. Be sure to remove the scum from the broth as it rises to the top with a skimming spoon designed for that purpose. Scum has no place in your broth.

7. When the broth is ready and has cooled somewhat, strain it through a fine mesh stainless steel strainer into quart sized Mason jars, then refrigerate overnight. The fat will rise to the top, solidify, and act as a seal that will help preserve the broth. Remove the fat before heating the broth.

8. Fresh broth should be kept in the refrigerator and used within a week of the time it is made. It is safest to bring the broth to a full boil when reheating it.

9. Use the proper equipment. You'll need a large stainless steel stockpot, a large stainless steel skimmer, lots of quart sized Mason jars, and a fine mesh stainless steel strainer that covers the opening of a Mason jar.

Bones, Gristle, and Other Scraps: Gold for Your Broth

Good bones are the basis of good broth. When properly simmered, the substances that come out of the bones not only fill the broth with nutrition, but provide wonderful taste and a depth of flavor. One of these substances is collagen, which turns into natural gelatin, providing essential health benefits, while binding the flavors in the broth together. Another great source of collagen is sinew — it melts right into the broth during the long simmering process.

It is often necessary to trim off gristle, sinew, and membranes when preparing grassfed meats. I used to get annoyed at the amount of gristle and sinew I had to trim off, before I learned how good it could be for broth. Now, I save every bit I trim, and freeze it until the next broth. The bones from a prime rib, the carcass of a roast chicken, all meat trimmings, the bones from short ribs, T-bones — all receive the same treatment. I used to throw all these trimmings out. Now, they provide the basis for wonderful broths.

Broth is beautiful.

Beef Broth

For centuries, many traditional European peoples have believed that beef gives strength. If they were peasants, they meant beef broth because the meat itself was far too expensive for them. However, the bones, sinews, and scraps were often available and were made into nourishing broth. Beef broth does give strength as well as a host of life-giving nutrients. It is warming, flavorful, and revitalizing. It adds tremendous flavor to pot roasts, pan roasts, stews, sauces, and gravies.

You will need a large stockpot for this one. Make sure that it is stainless steel, not aluminum. The long cooking time is necessary to combine the flavors, and get the nutrients out of the bones.

Makes 6 to 8 quarts

4 to 6 pounds assorted beef bones, scraps and trimmings, cartilage and sinew, including some marrow bones. Beef oxtails are ideal. Leftover bones from roasts are fine.

Enough filtered water to cover the bones by 2 to 3 inches

½ cup raw organic apple cider vinegar

Assorted Root Vegetables

1 large organic onion, peeled and coarsely chopped

4 stalks of organic celery, coarsely chopped

4 large organic carrots, peeled and coarsely chopped

4 cloves organic garlic, peeled and coarsely chopped

For Simmering

1 bunch organic Italian parsley, each stalk cut into 2 or 3 pieces

2 tablespoons coarse unrefined sea salt

1. Put the beef into a large stainless steel stockpot. Add the water and the vinegar. Let sit at room temperature for 1 hour.

2. Add all the vegetables, except the parsley. Heat the pot until the water begins a strong simmer. This will take a while due to the large volume of ingredients and water.

3. When the water is close to boiling, remove all the scum that rises to the top with a skimming spoon. This can also take a while, but is necessary.

4. Once the scum is gone, add the parsley and the salt.

5. Cover and simmer gently for 12 to 14 hours.

6. Using a ladle, strain into jars, cover, and refrigerate once the bottles have cooled down. The fat will rise to the top, and will solidify in the refrigerator. This fat cap will help preserve the broth. The fat should be removed before the broth is reheated. It can be used as cooking fat in all kinds of dishes.

Bison Broth

Bison are huge powerful animals with strong bones. I have found bison meat to be refreshing and revitalizing, so I thought that bison would make great broth. All good broths should be based on bones, sinew, and cartilage. I was delighted to find bison bones that were ideal for soup making. This broth is full of the health-giving qualities of bison. It has a subtle flavor which is quite refreshing. It works great as the liquid for a bison pot roast or stew, but we like to drink this broth so much, that it is rare for us to have any left over for gravies and stews.

You will need a large stockpot for this one. Make sure that it is stainless steel, not aluminum. The long cooking time is necessary to combine the flavors, and get the nutrients out of the bones.

Makes 6 to 8 quarts

4 pounds assorted bison bones with cartilage and meat. Bison oxtails are excellent.

Enough filtered water to cover the bones by 2 to 3 inches

½ cup raw organic apple cider vinegar

Assorted Root Vegetables

1 large organic onion, peeled and coarsely chopped

4 stalks of organic celery, coarsely chopped

4 large organic carrots, peeled and coarsely chopped

For Simmering

1 bunch of organic Italian parsley, each stalk cut into 2 or 3 pieces

2 tablespoons coarse unrefined sea salt

1. Put the bison into a large stainless steel stockpot. Add the water and the vinegar. Let sit at room temperature for 1 hour.

2. Add all the vegetables, except the parsley. Heat the pot until the water begins a strong simmer. This will take a while due to the large volume of ingredients and water.

3. When the water is close to boiling, remove all the scum that rises to the top with a skimming spoon. This can also take a while, but is necessary. For some reason, bison seems to have even more scum to be removed than other meats. It's worth the extra work.

4. Once the scum is gone, add the parsley and the salt.

5. Cover and simmer gently for 12 to 14 hours.

6. Using a ladle, strain into jars, cover, and refrigerate once the bottles have cooled down. The fat will rise to the top, and will solidify in the refrigerator. This fat cap will help preserve the broth. The fat should be removed before the broth is reheated. It can be used as cooking fat in all kinds of dishes.

Lamb Broth

Lamb broth is unusual in America, but is well loved throughout the world. Some people are afraid that it would taste too strong or gamy. This one is absolutely delicious and nourishing. Don't be put off by the large amount of garlic. Garlic and lamb are traditional partners in taste, and complement each other perfectly in this broth. The vinegar and vegetables bring out the best flavors. Grassfed American lamb has a clean fresh taste. This broth is a great way to use the leftover bones from your lamb roasts, and is very refreshing.

You will need a large stockpot for this one. Make sure that it is stainless steel, not aluminum. The long cooking time is necessary to combine the flavors, and get the nutrients out of the bones.

Makes 6 to 8 quarts

4 to 5 pounds assorted lamb bones with cartilage and some meat. Leftover bones from lamb roasts are ideal.

Enough filtered water to cover the bones by 2 to 3 inches

½ cup raw organic apple cider vinegar

Assorted Root Vegetables

1 bulb of garlic, peeled

1 large organic onion, peeled and coarsely chopped

4 stalks of organic celery, coarsely chopped

4 large organic carrots, peeled and coarsely chopped

For Simmering

1 bunch of organic Italian parsley, each stalk cut into 2 or 3 pieces

2 tablespoons coarse unrefined sea salt

1. Put the lamb into a large stainless steel stockpot. Add the water and the vinegar. Let sit at room temperature for 1 hour.

2. Add all the vegetables, except the parsley. Heat the pot until the water begins a strong simmer. This will take a while due to the large volume of ingredients and water.

3. When the water is close to boiling, remove all the scum that rises to the top with a skimming spoon. This can also take a while, but is necessary.

4. Once the scum is gone, add the parsley and the salt.

5. Cover and simmer gently for 12 to 14 hours.

6. Using a ladle, strain into jars, cover, and refrigerate once the bottles have cooled down. The fat will rise to the top, and will solidify in the refrigerator. This fat cap will help preserve the broth. The fat should be removed before the broth is reheated. It can be used as cooking fat in all kinds of dishes.

Chicken Broth

Chicken broth has been known for its healing properties for centuries. It has even been called "Jewish Penicillin." This particular broth is even more nourishing because the ingredients are processed and cooked so as to release even more of their nutrients into the soup. This broth can be used as the base for many sauces and soups. It can be used as the base for mashed potatoes, and as the cooking liquid for any kind of grain, such as rice, wheat, kasha, etc. It will make anything taste better. It is loaded with nutrients, minerals, gelatin, and other substances that add great flavor (as well as nutrition) to any dish.

You will need a large stockpot for this one. Make sure that it is stainless steel, not aluminum. The long cooking time is necessary to combine the flavors, and get the nutrients out of the bones.

Makes 6 to 8 quarts

5 to 6 pounds assorted free range chicken parts and bones, such as wing tips, backs, necks, carcasses from a roast chicken, legs, wings, etc.
Enough filtered water to cover the bones by 2 to 3 inches
½ cup raw organic apple cider vinegar

Assorted Root Vegetables
1 large organic onion, peeled and coarsely chopped
4 stalks of organic celery, coarsely chopped
4 large organic carrots, peeled and coarsely chopped
4 cloves of organic garlic, peeled and coarsely chopped

For Simmering
Several chicken giblets
1 bunch of organic Italian parsley, each stalk cut into 2 or 3 pieces
2 tablespoons coarse unrefined sea salt

1. Put the chicken into the pot, except for the giblets. Add the water and the vinegar. Let sit at room temperature for 1 hour.

2. Add all the vegetables, except the parsley. Heat the pot until the water begins a strong simmer. This will take a while due to the large volume of ingredients and water.

3. When the water is close to boiling, remove all the scum that rises to the top with a skimming spoon. This can also take a while, but is necessary.

4. Once the scum is gone, add the giblets, parsley, and the salt.

5. Cover and simmer gently for 12 to 14 hours.

6. Using a ladle, strain into jars, cover, and refrigerate once the bottles have cooled down. The fat will rise to the top, and will solidify in the refrigerator. This fat cap will help preserve the broth. The fat should be removed before the broth is reheated.

Turkey Broth

This broth is THE solution for leftover turkey, for all of it. The leftover turkey bones become a valued asset, contributing minerals, natural gelatin, and many nutrients. I always save the turkey drumsticks for this broth, as the drumstick's meat and many tendons transform into a wonderful gelatin in the broth. You can also use turkey wings, which are often sold separately. Turkey wings are wonderful for broth due to their high natural gelatin content. Turkey broth, much like chicken broth, is delicious and nourishing.

You will need a large stockpot for this one. Make sure that it is stainless steel, not aluminum. The long cooking time is necessary to combine the flavors, and get the nutrients out of the bones.

Makes 6 to 8 quarts

Leftover bones and carcass from a roasted turkey, or 4 to 6 pounds turkey wings
Turkey neck, (if available)
Enough filtered water to cover the bones by 2 to 3 inches
½ cup raw organic apple cider vinegar

Assorted Root Vegetables
1 large organic onion, peeled and coarsely chopped
4 stalks of organic celery, coarsely chopped
4 large organic carrots, peeled and coarsely chopped
4 cloves of organic garlic, peeled and coarsely chopped

For Simmering
Several chicken giblets
Turkey giblets, (if available)
1 bunch of organic Italian parsley, each stalk cut into 2 or 3 pieces
2 tablespoons coarse unrefined sea salt

1. Put the turkey into the pot, except for the giblets. Add the water and the vinegar. Let sit at room temperature for 1 hour.

2. Add all the vegetables, except the parsley. Heat the pot until the water begins a strong simmer. This will take a while due to the large volume of ingredients and water.

3. When the water is close to boiling, remove all the scum that rises to the top with a skimming spoon. This can also take a while, but is necessary.

4. Once the scum is gone, add the giblets, parsley, and the salt.

5. Cover and simmer gently for 12 to 14 hours.

6. Using a ladle, strain into jars, cover, and refrigerate once the bottles have cooled down. The fat will rise to the top, and will solidify in the refrigerator. This fat cap will help preserve the broth. The fat should be removed before the broth is reheated.

Nomad's Broth

The nomads of Eastern Europe roamed the Steppes in ancient times, depending on their flocks and hunting for their nourishment. The ancient writers tell us that these were some of the healthiest, strongest, and hardiest people the world has ever known. One of these groups, the Magyars, eventually settled in Hungary, adopted European civilization, and learned how to write. They recorded some details of what they ate while they were still nomads. Their most common food, made whenever they were not on the move, was a broth made in a huge iron pot known as a bogracs. The pot was filled with a good quantity of water, brought to a simmer over a fire, and filled with all kinds of food, including the bones, nutritious organs, and other parts of every animal brought in by the hunters or taken from the flocks, as well as whatever vegetables could be gathered in the locality. Everything went into the pot and was simmered together, resulting in an extremely nourishing broth.

The following is my modern version of this broth. The idea is to combine the meat and bones of several different animals, as well as some vegetables, so all these different nutrients can combine into a nourishing broth with a delicious combination of flavors. You will need a large stockpot for this one. Make sure that it is stainless steel, not aluminum. The long cooking time is necessary to combine the flavors, and get the nutrients out of the bones.

Makes 6 to 8 quarts

5 to 6 pounds assorted meat scraps and bones, from as many different sources as you have. This can include leftovers from roasts, meat trimmings, carcasses, and parts. A typical combination for me would be: some beef marrow bones; a carcass from a roast chicken; the bones from a lamb roast; chicken backs and necks; beef short ribs or oxtails. I have also used the carcass from a roast turkey and/or a roast duck.

Enough filtered water to cover the bones by 2 to 3 inches

½ cup raw organic apple cider vinegar

Assorted Root Vegetables

1 large organic onion, peeled and coarsely chopped

4 stalks of organic celery, coarsely chopped

4 large organic carrots, peeled and coarsely chopped

4 cloves of organic garlic, peeled and coarsely chopped

For Simmering

2 tablespoons coarse unrefined sea salt

1. Put the bones and scraps of meat in the pot. Add the water and the vinegar. Let sit at room temperature for 1 hour.

2. Add all the vegetables. Heat the pot until the water begins a strong simmer. This will take a while due to the large volume of ingredients and water.

3. When the water is close to boiling, remove all the scum that rises to the top with a skimming spoon. This can also take a while, but is necessary.

4. Once the scum is gone, add the salt.

5. Cover and simmer gently for 12 to 14 hours.

6. Using a ladle, strain into jars, cover, and refrigerate once the bottles have cooled down. The fat will rise to the top, and will solidify in the refrigerator. This fat cap will help preserve the broth. The fat should be removed before the broth is reheated. It can be used as cooking fat in all kinds of dishes.

Quadruple Healing Broth

Many traditional peoples have known about the healing power of broth and certain vegetables. The fabled healing power of Jewish chicken soup has been supported by several research studies.

In this recipe, we combine an improved chicken soup with four vegetables that traditional peoples have relied on for healing and better health.

The Egyptians were strong believers in the virtues of onions. The Chinese were great believers in the healing powers of green onions. The Welsh made the leek their national vegetable due to its health-giving qualities. Garlic has been valued for its healing qualities by many European peoples, including the Italians, the Poles, the Russians, and many others.

This recipe combines them all. It not only tastes great, but also nourishes and heals.

You will need a large stockpot for this one. Make sure that it is stainless steel, not aluminum. The long cooking time is necessary to combine the flavors, and get the nutrients out of the bones.

Makes 6 to 8 quarts

4 to 6 pounds assorted free range chicken parts and bones, such as wing tips, backs, necks, carcasses from a roast chicken, legs, wings, etc.

Enough filtered water to cover the bones by 2 to 3 inches

½ cup organic, raw, unfiltered apple cider vinegar

Assorted Root Vegetables

1 large organic leek, carefully washed, and chopped

1 large or 2 medium organic onions, peeled and chopped

1 bunch organic green onions, roots trimmed off, chopped

1 bulb of organic garlic, peeled and slightly crushed

For Simmering

Several chicken giblets

½ bunch organic Italian parsley, including stems, each stalk cut in half

2 tablespoons coarse unrefined sea salt

1. Peeling and crushing a whole bulb of garlic may seem like a lot of work. It is actually quite easy with the proper technique. You need a heavy cleaver or rolling pin. Separate the garlic cloves out of the bulb. Place the clove on a wooden cutting board, and press down hard on it with a rolling pin, or the flat of a cleaver. The clove will crack, and the skin will pop off easily. You may need to make one small cut at the root end of the clove to remove the remaining skin.

2. Put the bones and scraps of meat in the pot, except for the giblets. Add the water and the vinegar. Let sit at room temperature for 1 hour.

3. Add all the vegetables. Heat the pot until the water begins a strong simmer. This will take a while due to the large volume of ingredients and water.

4. When the water is close to boiling, remove all the scum that rises to the top with a skimming spoon. This can also take a while, but is necessary.

5. Once the scum is gone, add the giblets, parsley, and the salt.

6. Cover and simmer gently for 12 to 14 hours.

7. Using a ladle, strain into jars, cover, and refrigerate once the bottles have cooled down. The fat will rise to the top, and will solidify in the refrigerator. This fat cap will help preserve the broth. The fat should be removed before the broth is reheated.

Tender
Grassfed Beef

Judging Doneness in Grassfed Beef

Not all grassfed beef is the same. Different producers raise different breeds and crossbreeds. The plants which the cattle graze upon differ greatly from region to region, as does the quality of the soil. Some producers try to raise cattle with good fat content, others try to raise very lean cows. Some producers dry age their meat, some wet age it, and others do not age it at all. If the beef is aged, the aging period can vary from a few days to a month, or even more.

All of these variables affect the taste, tenderness, and cooking time of the meat. The cooking times given in this book are an estimate, based on experience. This is why variable times are given for so many recipes. These times should give excellent results for most grassfed beef. Do not be afraid to change the cooking times, based on your experience. You must get a feel for your cooking equipment, your oven, and the particular kind of beef you are cooking.

Judging Doneness

If you are cooking a roast, a good quality instant read meat thermometer can really help you judge the doneness of the meat, and how fast it is cooking. The ease with which the thermometer goes into the meat can also give you a good idea of how tender the meat is.

Doneness for Grassfed Beef:	
Rare	115 - 120 degrees
Medium Rare	121 - 130 degrees
Medium	131 - 140 degrees
Well Done	141 degrees and up

A meat thermometer does not work for steaks, because the meat is not thick enough.

Another way of judging temperature is to stick a metal skewer or roasting fork into the meat, withdraw it, and test the temperature of the metal with your finger. If it is cool, the meat is not ready. If it is somewhat warm, it is rare. If it is slightly hot, it is medium rare. If it is hot, it is medium. Once you have enough experience at comparing the temperature of the metal with the doneness of the meat, you will know how done the meat is, according to your standards.

The ease with which the skewer or fork goes into the meat will give you a good idea of its tenderness.

Many cooking authorities will tell you to never pierce the meat while cooking, or you will "lose valuable juices." I have never found this to be true. Yes, sometimes some juice comes out, but it does not hurt the taste or juiciness of the meat.

How to Cook a Tender, Delicious, Grassfed Steak: The Basics

This is the basic technique for cooking grassfed steaks and having them come out terrific. This technique will work beautifully with just about any steak. The technique is simple and easy. If you follow these steps with good grassfed beef, you will have a great steak.

1. **Grassfed is different.** Forget everything you ever knew about cooking steak.

2. **Get the proper equipment.** This means a well-seasoned, cast iron frying pan with a flat surface. (Not one of those ridged surfaces.) There is no real substitute, but you can get good results with a heavy bottomed pan, as long as you do not use a non-stick pan.

3. **Get the proper ingredients.** Besides the meat, you need these three:

   a. **Unfiltered, organic, extra virgin olive oil.** There is no good substitute. It should be unfiltered for proper marination. The unfiltered oil contains enzymes and other substances which make the meat more tender and bring out its flavor. Filtered oil is a mediocre substitute.

   b. **Natural, unrefined sea salt,** such as Celtic Sea Salt®, RealSalt®, or other salt of this nature. Whatever you do, do NOT use refined salt.

   c. **Pastured organic butter.** The type of butter you use is crucial to success. It should be a butter that is not watery, a butter that will not burn at medium heat, a butter that IS real butter. You could use a European style butter, but it will not taste as good. If you don't want to use butter, you could use beef tallow, unhydrogenated lard, extra virgin olive oil, or unrefined, extra virgin coconut oil, (no other vegetable oil should be used). Do not even consider the use of supermarket butters, as these are watery, contain additives, and will ruin the steak.

4. **Get the proper cut of grassfed steak.** This can be boneless or bone in.

Boneless Cuts:	Bone In Cuts:
Center cut shoulder	Bone in New York or strip
Cross rib	Delmonico
Filet	Porterhouse
Flat iron	Rib
Hanger	T-bone
New York	
Ribeye	
Sirloin	
Strip	
Tenderloin	
Top sirloin	
Tri-tip	

The thickness of these steaks should be approximately ¾ to 1½ inches. Most steaks are within this range.

How to Sauté a Steak

When I use the word "sauté" in a recipe, I mean cooking with some fat in a cast iron frying pan over medium heat.

1. The night before you plan to cook the steak, coat all sides with unfiltered, organic, extra virgin olive oil. (Remember, it should be unfiltered.) Depending on the size of the steaks, 2 to 4 tablespoons should be enough. Place in a glass bowl. Let sit for 1 hour, cover, and refrigerate overnight.

2. At least 1 hour before you plan to cook the steak, remove the steak from the refrigerator so it can come to room temperature. Room temperature means that the steak is cool to the touch, not cold. (Cooking a cold steak will result in tough meat.)

3. Heat 2 tablespoons pastured butter in a cast iron frying pan over medium heat. That's right, the heat never goes above medium.

4. When the butter is hot, bubbly, and slightly smoking, quickly sprinkle the salt lightly over both sides of the steak, then put the steak in the pan.

5. Cook for 3 to 5 minutes, (depending on how rare you want it). Then turn it over and cook for another 3 to 5 minutes.

That's all there is to it. You should have a nicely browned, juicy, tender steak that is just bursting with flavor, and a joy to eat.

Timing

The cooking time is based on a 1 inch steak, and should produce a steak that is medium rare at 4 minutes to a side, and rare at 3 minutes to a side. If you want it really rare, 2 minutes to a side may be enough. If you want it more medium and pink, 5 minutes to a side should do the trick.

A thinner steak will take less time, a thicker steak will take more time. In other words, a 1½ inch steak might take 5 minutes on a side to reach medium rare, while a ¾ inch steak might take 2 minutes on a side. All burners are unique in the exact amount of heat they generate, so pay attention to what happens with your stove and your pan. Don't hesitate to adjust the times to conform with the heat generated by your burner.

Simple Broiled Steak

Most of the steak recipes in this book are pan broiled or pan sautéed. These are great ways to make a steak. However, there are other methods to make a perfectly good steak. One method, the barbecue, is so vast a subject as to deserve its own book. Another method, oven broiling, is used here.

Oven broiling is tricky because you have to turn the heat high enough that the broiling element will stay on throughout the entire cooking process. The oven broiler must be used with the oven door partially open, which prevents the oven from getting too hot. Many cooks dislike oven broiling because the broiler does not get hot enough. Some restaurants have custom-made broilers that create and maintain an enormous blast of heat as high as 1700 degrees. While really high heat may be necessary to cook watery factory meat, a lower heat works just fine for grassfed meat.

The way to achieve the correct temperature for oven broiling grassfed meat is simple.

1. Bring the oven rack up to the 2nd highest position. (Please note that the meat should be approximately 4 inches below the broiler element.)
2. Lightly grease a broiler rack which is set in a pan.
3. Turn the oven to "Broil," and the heat to "Broil."
4. Place the broiler rack and pan on the oven rack. Let it heat for 5 minutes with the oven door partially open.
5. Place the meat on the preheated broiler rack.

Just about any tender steak can be broiled by this method, as long as it is not too thick. The following recipe will give you a good steak.

Serves 4

4 strip steaks, 1 to 1½ inches thick, about 2 pounds total

For the Marinade
2 tablespoons unfiltered organic extra virgin olive oil

For Broiling
2 tablespoons melted butter, (or melted beef tallow)

1. At least 1 hour before you plan to cook the meat, rub the olive oil all over the steaks. Let rest at room temperature for 1 hour.
2. Preheat the broiler as described above.
3. When the broiler is preheated, place the steaks on the broiler rack. Do not overcrowd the steaks. Put the broiler back in the oven. Cook for 2 minutes.
4. Turn the steaks over, and cook for 2 more minutes.
5. Remove the steaks from the oven, and brush all surfaces with melted butter (or melted beef tallow). Return the steaks to the broiler and cook for 2 minutes more on each side.
6. The steaks should be medium to medium rare, with a nice beefy flavor.

Serve and enjoy.

Butter Brushed Porterhouse Steak

Porterhouse is one of the most honored steaks in America. It has been called the king of steaks, and was immortalized by Mark Twain as the "Mighty Porterhouse Steak." This cut unites the pleasures of strip loin and tenderloin in one steak. The flavor of both is enhanced by the T shaped bone that divides them. T-bone steak is essentially the same cut, although it usually has a smaller portion of tenderloin.

The bone, which adds so much flavor and succulence, also makes the steak unsuitable for sautéing. The problem is the central location of part of the bone, which acts like a rack, and can prevent part of the meat from touching the pan.

My solution is to broil the steak. Here, we marinate the meat with a simple, flavorful mixture of garlic, olive oil, green onions, and pepper, then brush it with butter as it cooks. The result? A tender, delicious steak, made even better by the bone.

Serves 2 to 4

2 Porterhouse (or T-bone) steaks, 1 to 1¼ inches thick

For the Marinade
2 tablespoons unfiltered organic extra virgin olive oil
2 cloves organic garlic
2 organic green onions
1 teaspoon freshly ground organic black pepper

For Broiling
2 tablespoons pastured butter
1 teaspoon coarse unrefined sea salt, crushed

1. Rub the olive oil into all sides of the steaks. Crush the garlic and green onions, chop small, and press into all sides of the steaks. Sprinkle the pepper over all sides of the steaks. Let rest for 1 hour at room temperature.

2. Melt the butter, and keep warm.

3. Bring the oven rack up to the 2nd highest position. (Please note that the meat should be approximately 4 inches below the broiler element.)

4. Lightly grease a broiler rack which is set in a pan. Turn the oven to "Broil," and the heat to "Broil." Place the broiler rack and pan on the oven rack. Let it heat for 5 minutes with the oven door partially open.

5. Scrape the marinade off the steaks, and discard. Place the steaks on the preheated broiler rack.

6. Cook for 2 minutes. Turn the steaks over, and cook for 2 more minutes.

7. Remove the steaks from the oven, brush each side with melted butter, then sprinkle each side with the salt. Return to the oven and cook for 2 to 3 minutes on each side, depending on the thickness of the steaks and how you like them.

Serve, and enjoy these mighty steaks.

Giant Bone In Rib Steak with Secret Seasoning Salt

There is nothing in the food world quite as impressive and desired as a huge, thick, juicy, tender steak. Such a steak is even better when it is on the bone. The bone gives tremendous flavor and seems to make the meat even more juicy and tender. It can be hard to find a really thick, bone in, grassfed steak. You can create such a steak by cutting a bone in prime rib evenly along the line of the bones, so each bone is attached to a big, thick expanse of meat that is about the same thickness as the bone. I understand this cut is very popular in Argentina, where they know a thing or two about grassfed beef.

This is one of those times where I break my own rule about simple seasoning. I break the rule because this seasoning salt goes really well with this magnificent cut of beef. This is a special, wonderful steak for true beef lovers. I'll let you decide how many people this steak serves.

For Each Steak
    1 bone in steak cut from the prime rib, (about 1½ to 2 inches thick)
    2 tablespoons unfiltered organic extra virgin olive oil
    2 teaspoons *Secret Seasoning Salt* (page 186), crushed
    2 tablespoons pastured butter

1. Take the steak out of the refrigerator at least 1 hour before you plan to cook it. Rub the olive oil into the meat. (It would be even better to marinate the meat the day before you plan to cook it, and refrigerate it overnight. Remember to take the meat out of the refrigerator at least 1 hour before cooking.)

2. Melt the butter over medium heat in a cast iron frying pan. While the butter is melting, rub the **Secret Seasoning Salt** over both sides of the meat, covering each side evenly. When the butter is hot and slightly smoking, place the steak in the pan, and let it cook for 5 minutes. Turn the steak over, and cook for another 5 minutes.

3. Turn the heat down to medium low, and cook the steak for 2 to 5 minutes on each side, depending on how rare you want it. Do not overcook.

This is one of the ultimate meat experiences. Enjoy!

Twice Cooked Prime Rib Steak

Another way to tenderize grassfed beef is to cook it in two stages. Pre-browning the meat and letting it rest begins a process that results in tender, flavorful meat. This is a common technique in restaurants, though it is almost always used with factory beef. It is so much better with grassfed beef.

I've chosen a bone in prime rib steak for this recipe. The bone provides great flavor and juiciness, while the prime rib's fat helps keep it tender and delicious.

Some people think that you can't have a thick, tender, grassfed steak. They couldn't be more wrong, as you will find out.

Serves 2 to 4

1-rib prime rib roast with bone attached, 1½ to 2 inches thick
2 tablespoons pastured butter

1. Let the meat come to room temperature at least 1 hour before cooking.

2. Melt the butter over medium heat in a cast iron frying pan. When the butter is hot and slightly smoking, brown the meat in the pan. The goal is to get it brown on each side, not scorched. When browned, remove the meat from the pan, and place it on a rack.

3. Let the meat rest for 2 hours at room temperature. Do not wash the frying pan in which you browned the meat, because you'll be using it later. Leave it just the way it is.

4. After the meat has rested, reheat the fat in the frying pan, using medium heat. The butter in the pan may be brown at this point, and there'll be delicious little brown bits mixed in with it. When the fat is hot and slightly smoking, put the meat back in the pan.

5. Cook it for 3 minutes on each side, if you want it really rare. 4 minutes on each side, if you want it medium rare. 5 minutes on each side, if you want it medium.

6. No matter what timing you use, the exterior of the meat should be a deep beautiful brown. Remove the meat from the pan when done.

Get ready for steak heaven.

Tender, Sautéed Ribeye Steak

Grassfed beef can be wonderfully tender, if properly cooked. It must be cooked differently than grainfed beef. Success is in the details. Follow this recipe carefully, and you will end up with a tender, delicious steak.

Serves 3 to 4

Several ribeye steaks, about 2 pounds, cut ½ inch thick

For the Marinade
2 tablespoons unfiltered organic extra virgin olive oil

For Sautéing
1 teaspoon coarse unrefined sea salt, crushed
Freshly ground organic black pepper
2 tablespoons pastured butter
2 tablespoons extra virgin olive oil

1. Coat the steaks on each side with the unfiltered olive oil. Use just enough oil to coat each side of each steak. Place the steaks in a dish, in a single layer. Marinate at room temperature for about 1 hour.

2. Season each side of each steak with crushed sea salt, and several grindings of pepper.

3. Heat the butter and olive oil in a cast iron frying pan over medium heat. Do not raise the heat above medium at any point in the cooking process.

4. When the butter is melted, and the mixture is hot and bubbly, put the steaks in the pan, in a single layer. Cook for exactly 2 minutes.

5. Turn the steaks over, and cook for 2 minutes more.

Serve immediately. The steaks should be tender, juicy, pink, and delicious.

Pan Grilled Ribeye
With the Flavor of Old California

A small group of Spaniards was given land grants by the king of Spain in what is now California. Many of these grants were huge, and they were used as ranches. Vast herds of cattle were raised, and they were the lifeblood of the economy. Cattle hides were the main product, and they would be sold once or twice a year to the ships that came from Spain. The beef was all grassfed, and was not particularly tender because the cattle were raised for their hides, not their meat. Despite this, the settlers, known as Californios, developed some distinctive, delicious ways of cooking the beef. The flavors they developed seemed ideal for grassfed steak. The results turned out even better than I hoped.

The Californios were much more likely to use salt instead of olive oil in their marinades. I have dumped the salt and added the olive oil. The result is a marinade that not only flavors the meat exquisitely, but makes it more tender. The oil really carries the flavors of the marinade deep into the meat. This one's a winner.

Serves 4

2 pounds ribeye steaks, 1 to 1½ inch thick

For the Marinade
4 cloves organic garlic, finely chopped

2 tablespoons minced fresh organic oregano

½ teaspoon smoked Spanish paprika, (or 1 teaspoon sweet Spanish paprika)

½ teaspoon freshly ground organic black pepper

3 tablespoons unfiltered organic extra virgin olive oil

For Sautéing
1 teaspoon coarse unrefined sea salt, crushed

2 tablespoons extra virgin olive oil

1. Mix all marinade ingredients together, making sure they are thoroughly combined. Rub the marinade on both sides of the steaks. Let sit for 1 hour at room temperature, then cover and refrigerate overnight.

2. Remove the meat from the refrigerator at least 1 hour before you plan to cook it, so it can come to room temperature.

3. Scrape the marinade off the steaks with a spoon. (It's all right if a few little bits stick to the steak, as long as you get most of it off.) Heat the olive oil in a cast iron frying pan over medium heat. Sprinkle the salt on both sides of the meat.

4. When the oil is hot, bubbly, and slightly smoking, sauté the steaks over medium heat for 3 to 4 minutes on each side. Remove the steaks from the pan, and let rest 2 to 4 minutes in a warm place. This should give you a steak that ranges from medium to rare, depending on how thick the steak is.

Serve, and savor the wonderful taste of Old California.

Steak in the Style of Ancient China

Chinese cuisine brings up thoughts of rice, vegetables, seafood, and a multitude of spices and flavors. Steaks are not normally thought of as part of Chinese cuisine. In ancient times, however, meat was the most prized food in China. The meat was flavored by cooking it in different animal fats. For example, pork might be fried in lamb fat, or duck fat. The use of different animal fats was done to vary the flavors of the meat.

While I have seen no detailed recipes, I was inspired by this ancient custom to sauté steak with various fats, and the results were just wonderful.

This recipe calls for duck fat, but it would be equally successful with natural pork lard, grassfed lamb tallow, goose fat, or bison fat. Each of these fats lends a different flavor to the meat. The only flavorings used here are the fat and a little salt. Nothing else is needed.

Serves 4

2 pounds ribeye steak, 1 to 1¼ inches thick

For the Marinade
2 tablespoons unfiltered organic extra virgin olive oil

For Sautéing
2 tablespoons rendered duck fat, (for a different flavor, substitute natural unhydrogenated pork lard, grassfed lamb tallow, goose fat, or bison fat)

1 teaspoon coarse unrefined sea salt, crushed

1. Coat the steaks with the unfiltered olive oil at least 1 hour before you plan to cook them. Let rest at room temperature for the hour.

2. Heat the fat over medium heat in a heavy bottomed frying pan until hot and slightly smoking.

3. Sprinkle the salt on the steaks, and place them in the pan. Cook for 3 to 5 minutes on each side, depending on their thickness, and how you like them done.

Serve and enjoy.

Twice Cooked Ribeye Steak

Boneless ribeye steak is one of America's favorite cuts of beef. When it is twice cooked with flavorful grassfed beef, and pastured butter — it is beyond good. The intense, juicy, beefy flavor of the tender ribeye is exquisite. Be warned — you may find it addictive.

Serves 3 to 6

For the Initial Browning
1 piece of boneless ribeye, 3 to 4 inches thick
2 tablespoons pastured butter

For Sautéing
1 teaspoon coarse unrefined sea salt, crushed
½ teaspoon freshly ground organic black pepper
2 tablespoons pastured butter

1. The day before you plan to cook the steaks, melt 2 tablespoons of butter in a cast iron frying pan over medium heat. When the butter is hot and slightly smoking, brown all sides of the meat, turning as needed. This should take from 6 to 10 minutes, depending on the size and shape of the meat. Be sure that every part of the meat is browned. When the meat is browned, put it on a plate, pour the pan drippings over it, and let rest at room temperature for 1 hour. After 1 hour, place it in a glass bowl, cover, and refrigerate.

2. Remove the bowl from the refrigerator 1 hour before you plan to cook the meat, so it can come to room temperature.

3. When the meat has reached room temperature, cut it into steaks with one of the following thicknesses: 1½ inches thick for rare steaks; 1 inch thick for medium rare steaks; ¾ inch thick for medium steaks.

4. Just before you are ready to cook the steaks, sprinkle them on both sides with the salt and pepper. Melt 2 tablespoons of butter over medium heat in a cast iron frying pan. When the butter is hot and slightly smoking, cook the steaks for 3 minutes on each side for rare to medium rare, or a little longer for medium. (The cooking time is less than usual, because the steaks were partially pre-cooked.)

Serve, and enjoy some of the most flavorful beef you will ever eat.

Sautéed Strip Steak with French Flavors

The strip loin, also known as New York steak, is one of the most popular, expensive, and flavorful cuts of beef. The strip loin is not quite as tender as some of the other prime cuts.

A good marinade can really enhance the tenderness. The marinade we have chosen for this recipe not only makes the steak tender, but really enhances the flavor.

I deliberately chose the French flavor marinade for this steak because I was curious to see how traditional French flavors would work with this cut. The French have few recipes for the strip loin, instead favoring tenderloin, ribeye, and other cuts. The results were absolutely delicious. The French don't know what they are missing.

Serves 4

3 pounds strip steaks, about 1 to 1½ inches thick

For the Marinade
1 small organic onion, coarsely chopped
1 large stalk organic celery, coarsely chopped
1 large organic carrot, coarsely chopped
2 cloves organic garlic, finely chopped
2 imported bay leaves, crushed
1 teaspoon fresh organic thyme leaves, finely chopped
6 sprigs organic Italian parsley, chopped
½ teaspoon freshly ground organic black pepper

For Sautéing
2 tablespoons pastured butter
1 teaspoon coarse unrefined sea salt, crushed

1. Crush all the ingredients for the marinade, and mix well.

2. Place the steak in a glass bowl, and rub the marinade all over the steaks. Let the steaks marinate at room temperature for 1 to 2 hours.

3. Scrape the marinade off the steaks.

4. Heat the butter over medium heat in a heavy bottomed pan. Sprinkle the salt over both sides of the steaks. When the butter is hot and slightly smoking, place the steaks in the pan, and cook for 3 to 5 minutes, depending on the thickness and how you like it.

5. Turn the steaks over, and cook for another 3 to 5 minutes.

Serve, and enjoy this superbly flavored steak.

Classic Tenderloin Steak

Tenderloin is one of the most valued cuts of beef. It is very lean and very tender. Many cooking authorities claim that tenderloin lacks flavor. Tenderloin is almost always heavily seasoned, or served with a sauce. While it is certainly true that factory tenderloin has little flavor, it is most certainly not true for grassfed tenderloin. The meat of grassfed tenderloin has real flavor.

The classic tenderloin filet is a circular piece of meat, cut from the thicker part of the tenderloin, about 1 to 1½ inches thick. Europeans like to top a tenderloin filet with a fried egg. This recipe celebrates the unique texture and superb flavor of grassfed tenderloin in the classic way, by sautéing it in good butter, yes, and topping it with the traditional egg.

Serves 4

4 tenderloin filets, 1 to 1½ inches thick

For the Marinade
2 tablespoons unfiltered organic extra virgin olive oil

For Sautéing
2 tablespoons pastured butter

1 teaspoon organic extra virgin olive oil

1 teaspoon coarse unrefined sea salt, crushed

1 teaspoon freshly ground organic black pepper

4 organic eggs

1. Coat the filets with the unfiltered olive oil at least 1 hour before you plan to cook it. Let rest at room temperature for the hour.

2. Heat the butter and extra virgin olive oil over medium heat in a heavy bottomed frying pan until hot and slightly smoking.

3. Sprinkle the salt and pepper on the filets, and place them in the pan. Cook for 3 to 5 minutes on each side, depending on their thickness, and how you like them done. They should not be cooked beyond medium rare. Remove the filets from the heat, and let rest in a warm place while you prepare the eggs.

4. Carefully break the eggs into the same pan you used for the steaks. Cook over medium heat, basting the yolks with the pan drippings, until done. The yolks should be soft and runny. Top each steak with an egg, and enjoy this classic.

Irish Whiskey Steak

The Irish love their fine grassfed steaks. They also appreciate their equally fine whiskey. I decided to combine the two, with delicious results. Whiskey can add a great flavor to grassfed steak. The olive oil helps keep the meat tender, while carrying the flavor of the whiskey into the meat. Jameson Irish whiskey is ideal for this recipe.

We have this every Saint Patrick's Day. This is a steak to celebrate with.

Serves 4

4 (8 ounce) top sirloin steaks, 1 to 1¼ inches thick

For the Marinade

3 tablespoons unfiltered organic extra virgin olive oil

2 tablespoons Irish whiskey, Jameson is ideal

3 organic green onions finely chopped

1 teaspoon freshly ground organic black pepper

For Sautéing

2 tablespoons pastured butter

1. The night before you plan to cook the steaks, combine the olive oil, whiskey, chopped green onions, and black pepper. Place the steaks in a glass bowl, coat with the marinade, cover, and refrigerate overnight.

2. Remove the steaks from the refrigerator 1 hour before you plan to cook them, so they can come to room temperature.

3. Scrape the marinade off the steaks with a spoon. (It's all right if a few little bits stick to the steak, as long as you get most of it off.) Heat the butter over medium heat in a heavy bottomed frying pan until hot and slightly smoking.

4. Cook for 3 to 5 minutes on each side, depending on their thickness, and how you like them done. They should not be cooked beyond medium rare.

Serve and enjoy.

Scottish Steak

No nation has been more successful at creating great beef cattle than Scotland. Two of the most famous heritage breeds developed in Scotland are the Aberdeen Angus and the Short Horn. Unfortunately for the Scots, their general poverty resulted in most of this fine beef being sent to England, where it formed the foundation of the famous English love of beef. Fortunately for the United States and Argentina, the Angus and the Short Horn were transported there to become the ancestors of the best beef herds in those nations.

The following recipe is based on old Scottish recipes for marinated steak. This steak will be delicious with any good grassfed beef. Or try it with some grassfed Angus beef in honor of the great Scottish cattle breeders who developed the world's best beef cattle.

Serves 4

1 (2 pound) ribeye steak, (or strip, or top sirloin), 1½ to 2½ inches thick

For the Marinade

3 tablespoons unfiltered organic extra virgin olive oil

1 large organic onion, sliced

Leaves from 1 medium sprig of fresh organic rosemary

1 large sprig organic sage, left whole

4 sprigs fresh organic thyme, left whole

1 sprig fresh organic oregano or marjoram, left whole

12 organic black peppercorns, left whole

2 organic bay leaves

For Sautéing

2 tablespoons pastured butter

1 teaspoon coarse unrefined sea salt, crushed

1. The night before you plan to cook the steak, rub it with the unfiltered olive oil. Put the steak in a glass bowl. Add the rest of the marinade ingredients to the bowl. Press the vegetables, herbs, and peppercorns into all sides of the meat. Let sit at room temperature for 1 hour, then cover and refrigerate overnight.

2. An hour before you plan to cook the steak, remove the bowl from the refrigerator. When the steak has reached room temperature, remove from the marinade, and scrape off any part of the marinade that is still on the steak. Sprinkle the salt over the steak just before you start cooking it.

3. Melt the butter in a cast iron frying pan over medium heat. When the butter is hot and slightly smoking, cook the steak for 5 minutes over medium heat on each side. Test for doneness. If the steak is not done, reduce the heat to low, and cook the steak for 2 minutes on each side. Test for doneness. If the steak is not done, continue cooking on low heat, testing frequently for doneness. Remember that grassfed meat cooks very quickly.

Serve, and enjoy this wonderful combination of flavors, and appreciate the fine beef created by the Scots.

Quick Garlic Parsley Steak

Garlic and parsley have been used together for ages. They are an honored part of Spanish and Latin American cuisine, and are also quite common all over the Mediterranean. Garlic and parsley make a great classic flavor combination for meat. Here, we add some pepper and unfiltered extra virgin olive oil which really carries the flavor deep into the meat. We also cut the steaks thin, so the maximum area is exposed to the marinade. The flavor is terrific, and thin steaks cook so quickly.

Serves 2

1 (1 pound) tenderloin or ribeye, cut into ½ inch slices

For the Marinade

¼ cup organic Italian parsley leaves, tightly packed

4 organic garlic cloves

1 teaspoon freshly ground organic black pepper

3 tablespoons unfiltered organic extra virgin olive oil

For Sautéing

2 tablespoons pastured butter

½ teaspoon coarse unrefined sea salt, crushed

1. The day before you plan to cook the steaks, prepare the marinade. Chop the garlic and parsley together until they are very finely chopped. Add the pepper and olive oil, and mix well. Rub the marinade all over the meat, let sit 1 hour at room temperature, then cover and refrigerate overnight. (If you're in a hurry, you can skip the overnight refrigeration, and just marinate it for 1 hour at room temperature.)

2. An hour before you plan to cook the steaks, remove the steaks from the refrigerator so they can reach room temperature.

3. When the steaks have reached room temperature, scrape the marinade off the steaks with a spoon. Sprinkle the salt on all sides.

4. Heat the butter over medium heat in a cast iron frying pan until it is hot and slightly smoking. Cook the steaks, without crowding, for a minute on each side. They should be medium rare to medium, and utterly delicious with the garlic parsley combination.

Polish Hungarian German Onion Steak

This recipe combines three traditional cooking techniques from three different countries. The combination of bacon fat and onions is traditional in all three countries, especially Hungary. We add unfiltered organic extra virgin olive oil, which really helps carry the flavor of the onion into the meat, while making the meat more tender. The magical combination of beef and onions is at its best in this recipe.

Serves 4

2 pounds strip steaks, (or ribeye, or top sirloin), cut 1 inch thick
2 tablespoons unfiltered organic extra virgin olive oil
2 large organic onions, peeled and sliced
6 slices fat, traditionally made bacon, (or ¼ cup pastured butter)
Freshly ground organic black pepper

1. Rub the steaks with the olive oil. Combine the onion slices with the steaks, making sure that every surface of each steak is covered with onions. Cover and refrigerate overnight, (or let sit for at least 2 hours at room temperature).

2. Place the bacon slices in an unheated, 12 inch cast iron frying pan. Turn the heat to medium.

3. Cook the bacon on medium, turning occasionally, until both sides are crisp and the bacon has rendered its fat. While the bacon is cooking, remove the steaks from the onion slices and wipe them dry. Wipe the onion slices dry also.

4. When the bacon is ready, remove it from the pan. Add the onions to the bacon fat, and cook over medium heat for 5 to 10 minutes, stirring occasionally, until the onions are soft and slightly brown.

5. Remove the onions from the pan with a slotted spoon, and reserve. The goal is to keep as much fat as possible in the pan.

6. Sprinkle the steaks with freshly ground black pepper to taste, and place in the hot bacon fat. Cook over medium heat for 3 to 5 minutes on each side, depending on how you like them done: 3 minutes on each side should give you rare; 4 minutes on each side should give you medium rare; and 5 minutes on each side should give you medium.

7. Cover the steaks with the reserved fried onions when you serve them.

This simple combination of ingredients provides a delicious, richly flavored steak in which the whole is much tastier than the sum of its parts.

Terrific Top Sirloin

A good thick steak is one of the most luxurious and delicious ways to experience grassfed beef. The thickness allows a variety of textures, juiciness, and states of doneness, ranging from a crisp, flavorful crust to a juicy, tender interior. This kind of steak was considered the ultimate in good eating by millions of people for hundreds of years, and has been celebrated in the literature of many countries. Top sirloin is loaded with flavor, and its texture is ideal for cooking a thick steak. This steak is actually the size of a small roast.

Serves 4

1 thick (2 to 2½ inches) top sirloin steak, about 2 to 2½ pounds

For the Marinade
2 tablespoons unfiltered organic extra virgin olive oil

For Sautéing
2 tablespoons pastured butter
***Secret Seasoning Salt* (page 186), (or coarse unrefined sea salt), crushed**

1. The day before you plan to cook the steak, rub all surfaces with the olive oil, place in a glass bowl, cover, and let sit for 1 hour. Refrigerate overnight. (If you want to cook it the same day, marinate it in the oil for 2 hours at room temperature.)

2. An hour before you plan to cook the steak, remove it from the refrigerator so it can come to room temperature.

3. When the meat has come to room temperature, heat the butter over medium heat in a cast iron frying pan. Rub the salt into both sides of the steak. When the butter is hot and slightly smoking, add the steak, and cook for 5 minutes over medium heat.

4. Turn the steak over, and cook for another 5 minutes on medium heat.

5. Reduce the heat to low, turn the steak over, and cook for another 5 minutes.

6. Turn the steak over, and cook for another 5 minutes on low. Test the steak for doneness. If it's rare in the middle, but warm, it will be medium rare as you move away from the middle to the sides, and medium near each surface of the steak. In other words, this steak is going to give you several degrees of doneness. If you wish the steak to be less rare, cook it on low for another 2 to 4 minutes on each side.

This is one of the ultimate beef experiences.

The Ultimate Onion Steak, Polish Style

European cooks have long loved to flavor meat with onions. This is especially true in Poland, where it is hard to find a traditional beef dish that is not flavored by onions in one way or another. Onion complements and brings out the flavor of good meat. This recipe celebrates the time-honored combination of steak and onions by using onions in three different ways to give a magnificent depth of flavor and tenderness.

Serves 4

1 large (2 pound) top sirloin steak, about 1½ inches thick

For the Marinade

2 tablespoons unfiltered organic extra virgin olive oil

1 medium organic onion, coarsely chopped, and crushed

1 teaspoon organic onion powder

For Sautéing

2 to 3 tablespoons pastured butter

1 medium organic onion, sliced

1 teaspoon coarse unrefined sea salt, crushed

1 teaspoon freshly ground organic black pepper

1. The night before you plan to cook the steak, place the steak in a glass bowl. Rub the olive oil all over the steak. Sprinkle the onion powder all over the steak. Surround the steak with the crushed onions, covering it on all sides. Let sit at room temperature for 1 hour, then cover and refrigerate overnight.

2. Remove the steak from the refrigerator 1 hour before you plan to cook it, so it can come to room temperature. When the steak is at room temperature, scrape off the onions, and reserve.

3. Heat 2 tablespoons butter over medium heat until it is hot and slightly smoking. Add the reserved onion and the sliced onion to the pan. Cook over medium heat until the onions are soft and lightly browned.

4. Remove the onions from the pan with a slotted spoon. You should have enough butter left in the pan to coat the pan's surface. If not, add another tablespoon of butter. Sprinkle the steak with salt and pepper. Leaving the heat at medium, add the steak, and cook for 3 to 5 minutes on each side, depending on the thickness and how you like it.

5. When the steak is done, let rest in a warm place. Return the onions to the pan, and let them cook at medium for a couple of minutes.

Cover the steak with the sautéed onions and serve. You will taste why steak and onions are so popular.

Tender Sirloin Tip Steak, Twice Cooked

Sirloin tip is usually thought of as a cut suitable for stews, pot roasts, and slow oven roasts, not steak. This is especially true for grassfed sirloin tip, which many cooks consign to the crock pot. Sirloin tip is one of the most economical cuts. It is very lean, and has great flavor, but tenderness is the issue. The twice cooked method works beautifully here to tenderize the meat. This steak is tender and delicious, and so satisfying.

Serves 4 to 6

1 (2 to 3 pound) sirloin tip roast

For the Initial Browning
2 tablespoons pastured butter
Crushed coarse unrefined sea salt to taste
Freshly ground organic pepper to taste

For Sautéing
2 tablespoons pastured butter

1. The key is to brown the roast at least 2 hours before you plan to cook the steaks, (or the day before). Remove any strings or netting from the roast, and wipe it dry. Heat the butter over medium heat in a cast iron frying pan. When the butter is hot and slightly smoking, brown the roast on all sides, turning it regularly to avoid scorching. When the roast is browned, place it on a plate. Let it rest for 2 hours, (or let it rest about an hour until it has cooled, then refrigerate overnight in a covered glass bowl).

2. If you have refrigerated the roast, remove it from the refrigerator 1 hour before you plan to cook it, so it can come to room temperature. Slice the roast into slices 1 to 1½ inches thick.

3. Heat the butter over medium heat in a cast iron frying pan. Season the steak slices on both sides with salt and pepper.

4. When the butter is hot and slightly smoking, cook the steaks for 2 to 4 minutes on each side, depending on how thick they are and how you like them. Remember that they will cook faster because they have been partially pre-cooked. Do not crowd the steaks together in the pan. Cook in batches if necessary.

Serve and enjoy.

Steak Frite

This is a classic French steak which is traditionally served with pommes frite, which translates to fried potatoes, commonly known as French fries. The combination of steak and French fries is popular in America, even with inferior factory beef and potatoes fried in tasteless vegetable oil. It is so much better when it is the real thing — flavorful grassfed beef and beef tallow for the French fries. Beef tallow from grassfed cattle gives a wonderful beefy, nutty flavor to the potatoes.

This recipe is true to its French roots. We use a less tender cut of steak that has great flavor, and sauté it simply. However, we improve on the original by using an olive oil marinade for a more tender steak.

Serves 2 to 4

1 pound tri-tip steak, cut into several pieces, ½ inch thick

For the Marinade

2 tablespoons unfiltered organic extra virgin olive oil

For Sautéing

2 tablespoons pastured butter

1 tablespoon organic extra virgin olive oil

Coarse unrefined sea salt, crushed

Freshly ground organic black pepper

1. Combine the steaks with the unfiltered extra virgin olive oil in a glass bowl. Cover and let sit for at least 1 hour at room temperature, or refrigerate overnight.

2. If you refrigerated the steaks, take them out at least 1 hour before you plan to start cooking them.

3. Melt the butter in a cast iron frying pan over medium heat. Add the extra virgin olive oil to the butter. When the butter is hot and slightly smoking, sprinkle the steaks lightly with salt and pepper on each side, then put them into the frying pan.

4. Sauté the steaks over medium heat for 1½ to 2 minutes on each side, depending on how rare you want them.

Serve with **Old Fashioned French Fries**. (See recipe on page 198.)

Thick and Tender Cross Rib Steak

The cross rib, also known as center cut shoulder, or shoulder clod, is usually made into pot roasts, or condemned to the crock pot. I'll share a little secret with you — cross rib can make a terrific tender steak, with some of the deepest, beefiest flavor you are ever going to taste. In fact, my family eats more cross rib steaks than any other cut. I usually buy a roast and cut it into steaks. That way, I can get a really thick steak.

Thick steaks are a luxury, from the crusty outside to the juicy center, but are difficult to cook properly. The usual problem is that the outside is burned and the inside is raw. This often happens if you are cooking waterlogged factory meat. Happily, this problem does not exist with grassfed beef, since it cooks so much faster, and at a lower heat than the factory stuff.

Now, this cut requires a little more effort to get it tender, but you won't mind the effort once you taste the steak.

Serves 4

1 (2 to 3 pound) center cut shoulder steak, about 2 inches thick

For the Marinade

3 tablespoons unfiltered organic extra virgin olive oil

1 large organic onion, chopped and crushed

For Sautéing

2 tablespoons pastured butter

1 teaspoon coarse unrefined sea salt, crushed

Freshly ground organic black pepper to taste

1. Trim all silverskin and other connective tissue from the surface of the steak.

2. Rub the olive oil into all surfaces of the meat. Place the steak in a glass bowl. Cover the steak with the crushed onion and any juices from the onion. Turn the meat in the bowl so that all surfaces are covered by the onion. Let rest at room temperature for 1 hour, then cover and refrigerate overnight.

3. Remove the meat from the refrigerator about 1 hour before you plan to cook it, so it can come to room temperature. Brush the onions off the meat.

4. Heat the butter over medium heat in a heavy bottomed frying pan, preferably cast iron. When the butter is hot and slightly smoking, sprinkle the meat with salt and pepper, and put the steak in the pan. Cook for 5 minutes.

5. Turn the steak over, and cook for 5 minutes more. Remove the steak to a plate. Let the steak rest for 10 minutes to 1 hour.

6. Reheat the butter in the pan on medium heat. When the butter is hot and slightly smoking, place the steak in the pan, turn the heat down to low, and cook for 5 minutes on each side. This should give you a beautiful medium rare steak. If the steak is not done to your liking, cook it for a few more minutes over low heat, testing frequently for doneness.

Serve, and enjoy this thick, juicy, tender steak.

Fantastic Flat Iron Steak

The chuck has been traditionally used for pot roasts, stews, and ground beef, because it is a tough cut of meat. However, there is a small portion of each chuck which is quite tender, when properly prepared. Even though flat iron steaks are not a part of traditional European cuisine, traditional methods work great for this cut of meat. The fresh herb and garlic marinade really brings out the fine flavor of this meat.

Serves 4

4 flat iron steaks, about 1 inch thick

For the Marinade

¼ cup unfiltered organic extra virgin olive oil

4 large cloves of organic garlic, finely chopped

2 tablespoons organic fresh rosemary leaves, finely chopped

2 tablespoons organic fresh sage leaves, finely chopped

2 tablespoons organic Italian parsley leaves, finely chopped

For Sautéing

2 tablespoons pastured butter

1 teaspoon coarse unrefined sea salt, crushed

1. Combine all the ingredients for the marinade. Mix well. Coat all sides of the steak with the marinade. Let rest at room temperature for 1 hour, then cover and refrigerate overnight.

2. At least 1 hour before you plan to cook the steaks, take them out of the refrigerator and let them warm to room temperature.

3. When the steaks have reached room temperature, remove the steaks from the marinade and scrape any remaining marinade off the steaks with a knife or a spoon. Melt the butter over medium heat in a cast iron frying pan. Sprinkle the steaks lightly with salt on both sides.

4. When the butter is hot and slightly smoking, sauté the steaks over medium heat for 3 to 4 minutes on each side, depending on how you like it done. This cut of steak should not be cooked beyond medium rare.

Serve and enjoy.

Sautéed Hanger Steak

Hanger steak, also known as the hanging tender, used to be known as "the butcher's steak." It received that title because there is only one per animal, and because it was so good that the butcher would take it home for himself. Hanger steak is somewhat trendy at the moment. Cooked properly, it has some of the deepest and richest beef flavor you will ever taste, and is very juicy. Cooked wrong, it is very tough.

This cut provided more of a challenge than any steak I ever cooked. I used to cut it into small steaks so I could remove the large wad of gristle in the center. The little steaks gave off a lot of liquid while cooking, which prevented them from browning properly. I finally decided to leave the hanger steak whole. I also used yet another traditional way to tenderize steak. The results? A magnificently browned steak, crusty on the outside, juicy and tender on the inside, with a flavor which made me realize why the butcher kept this one for himself. Each bite is so satisfying.

Serves 2 to 4

1 hanger steak, left whole, any exterior membranes trimmed off

For the Marinade
2 tablespoons unfiltered organic extra virgin olive oil

For Sautéing
2 tablespoons pastured butter
½ teaspoon organic onion powder
½ teaspoon organic garlic powder

1. The night before you plan to cook the steak, rub it with the oil, let sit for 1 hour at room temperature, then cover and refrigerate overnight.

2. About an hour before you plan to cook the steak, remove it from the refrigerator, then melt the butter in a large pan over medium heat. As soon as the butter is melted, remove the pan from the heat, and quickly coat each side of the steak in the butter. You don't want to cook it, just coat it. The butter will solidify on the steak, which is expected. Let the steak sit in the butter for 1 hour, at room temperature.

3. Heat the butter remaining in the pan over medium heat. Sprinkle the onion and garlic powder on each side of the steak. When the butter is hot and slightly smoking, cook the steak for 3 minutes on each side. Reduce the heat to medium low, and cook for 2 to 3 minutes on each side, depending on how you like it and the thickness of the steak. Do not cook beyond medium rare.

4. When done, let rest for a couple of minutes. Slice against the grain (and don't serve the gristle).

Enjoy the magnificent, beefy flavor.

Best Steakhouse Steak Version One, with French Flavors

The first steakhouse in the United States may have been the original Delmonico's restaurant, founded in 1837. While originally a French restaurant, Delmonico's became famous for its steaks, reputed to be the very finest in the nation. Many other restaurants developed their own version of the best steak.

Since these steaks were totally grassfed, I decided that no book on tender grassfed meat could be complete without a recipe for this classic grassfed steak. Little did I know that there is a controversy over the cut of meat that was used for the Delmonico style steak. In fact, my research has discovered no less that nine different cuts that claim this title. I narrowed this list down to three different cuts, and made all three, using different techniques. Each one so delicious that I couldn't decide the winner, so I decided to place all three in the book.

Since the flavorings used by the original chefs have been lost in the mists of time, I have flavored each recipe differently. This version uses a bone in rib steak. Since many early steakhouses started out as French restaurants, I decided to use French flavors. The result? Magnifique!

Serves 2 to 4

1 bone in rib steak, cut 1½ to 2 inches thick

For the Marinade

1 small organic onion, coarsely chopped

1 stalk organic celery, taken from the interior of the bunch, coarsely chopped

1 large organic carrot, peeled and coarsely chopped

2 cloves organic garlic, peeled

1 teaspoon fresh organic thyme leaves, finely chopped

6 sprigs organic fresh parsley, with stems, coarsely chopped

2 imported bay leaves, crushed with your fingers

For Sautéing

2 tablespoons pastured butter

Coarse unrefined sea salt, crushed, (preferably French)

Freshly ground organic black pepper

1. The night before you plan to cook the steak, make the marinade. Crush the vegetables, garlic, thyme, and parsley together. Mix thoroughly with the bay leaves. Press the mixture into both sides of the steak, and place in a glass bowl. Let rest at room temperature for 1 hour, then cover and refrigerate overnight.

2. Remove the steak from the refrigerator about 1 hour before you plan to cook it, so it can come to room temperature. Once the steak has reached room temperature, scrape the vegetables off with a spoon.

3. Heat the butter in a heavy bottomed frying pan over medium heat. When the butter is hot and slightly smoking, quickly sprinkle salt and pepper over both sides of the steak, then put the steak in the pan. Cook 5 minutes on each side. Check for doneness.

4. If the steak is not done, turn the heat down to medium low, turn the steak over, and check for doneness in 2 minutes. Turn again, if necessary, and check for doneness in 2 minutes. If it still is not done, keep turning and checking the steak at 1 minute intervals, until it is done to your taste.

This is a truly wonderful steak.

Best Steakhouse Steak Version Two, with Italian Flavors

This recipe uses a bone in steak from the short loin, also known as bone in strip steak. Many believe this cut to be the true Delmonico style steak. The bone gives it great flavor, and the short loin is one of the most tender and tasty cuts of beef. Since Delmonico's first cook was Italian, as were the founders, I've chosen to use an Italian flavor marinade with this steak. Every other marinade in this book would work well with this superb piece of beef, but I had to choose one. The combination of this tender, flavorful cut and this marinade results in a tender, exquisite piece of beef.

Serves 2 to 4

2 to 4 bone in steaks from the short loin, (or bone in strip steaks, or bone in New York steaks), 1 to 1½ inches thick

For the Marinade

4 organic garlic cloves, coarsely chopped

Leaves from 1 large sprig of organic fresh rosemary, coarsely chopped

1 small organic onion, coarsely chopped

1 small stalk organic celery, taken from the inside of the bunch, coarsely chopped

½ small organic carrot, peeled and coarsely chopped

1 tablespoon organic celery leaves, coarsely chopped

1 tablespoon organic Italian parsley leaves (no stems), coarsely chopped

1 teaspoon organic black pepper, coarsely ground

3 tablespoons unfiltered organic extra virgin olive oil, (preferably from Italy)

For Sautéing

2 tablespoons extra virgin olive oil, (preferably from Italy)

1 to 2 teaspoons coarse unrefined sea salt, crushed

1. The night before you plan to cook the steaks, make the marinade. Crush the vegetables. Combine the vegetables with the pepper and unfiltered olive oil. Mix well. Rub the mixture all over the steaks. Place in a covered glass bowl. Let sit at room temperature for 1 hour, then refrigerate overnight.

2. Remove the steaks from the refrigerator 1 hour before you plan to cook them, so they can come to room temperature. When the steaks have reached room temperature, scrape the marinade off the steaks, and discard.

3. Heat the olive oil in a large, heavy bottomed frying pan over medium heat. When the oil is hot, sprinkle the salt on both sides of the steaks, and cook for 3 to 5 minutes on each side, depending on the thickness of the steak and the degree of doneness you prefer.

Serve, and enjoy this magnificent steak!

Best Steakhouse Steak Version Three, with American Flavors

This version of the best early steakhouse steak may be the closest to the original. This is a boneless strip steak, also called a New York steak. It is very simply seasoned, with the traditional American meat seasonings of salt and pepper, and depends on the excellent natural flavor of the meat. This is also a fine steak. I suggest that you try all three versions, and decide for yourself which one is the best steakhouse steak.

Serves 2

2 boneless strip steaks, cut 1 to 1½ inches thick

For the Marinade
2 tablespoons unfiltered organic extra virgin olive oil

For Sautéing
2 tablespoons pastured butter
1 teaspoon coarse unrefined sea salt, crushed
½ teaspoon freshly ground organic black pepper

1. The night before you plan to cook the steaks, rub the olive oil on all sides of the meat. Let sit 1 hour at room temperature. Cover and refrigerate overnight. (If you want to cook it the same day, you can just marinate it in the oil for 1 hour at room temperature.)

2. Remove the steaks from the refrigerator 1 hour before you plan to cook them, so they can come to room temperature.

3. Heat the butter over medium heat in a heavy bottomed pan until hot and slightly smoking.

4. Season the steaks on all sides with the salt and pepper. Cook for 3 to 5 minutes on each side, depending on the thickness of the meat and how you like the steaks.

Serve and enjoy.

English Style Prime Rib

The English have been famous for their prime rib for a long, long time. While the traditional recipes call for roasting a full seven-rib roast on a spit in front of a fire, we get excellent results with a two-rib roast and an oven. The olive oil, onion, garlic, and black pepper are not English, but really deepen the flavor. Why do we call it English style? We call it "English" because it is cooked at a fairly high heat throughout the cooking time.

This recipe breaks the rule about not cooking grassfed beef at high heat. For some reason, it comes out tender and juicy, with a deep beefy flavor that must be tasted to be believed.

Serves 4

2-rib bone in prime rib roast, with fat cap

For the Marinade
2 tablespoons unfiltered organic extra virgin olive oil
4 large organic garlic cloves, peeled, and coarsely chopped

For Roasting
Freshly ground organic black pepper

1. Remove the roast from the refrigerator at least 2 hours before you plan to cook it. Coat all meat surfaces with the olive oil. Press the garlic pieces into the meat surfaces, making sure that each meat surface is coated with some garlic. Let the roast sit for 2 hours at room temperature.

2. Preheat oven to 425 degrees. Put the roast in a roasting pan, bone side down. Remove the garlic from the meat surfaces, and place the garlic on top of the fat cap. Grind a generous coating of organic black pepper over the fat cap.

3. Place the roast in the preheated oven. Cook for 15 minutes.

4. Baste the roast with the fat in the pan. Cook for another 15 minutes.

5. Baste the roast with the fat in the pan for the second time. Cook for another 15 minutes.

6. Check for doneness with a meat thermometer. If the roast is not done to your taste, return to the oven, checking the temperature at 5 minute intervals.

Serve and enjoy.

High-Low Prime Rib with
Herb Garlic Marinade

Prime rib has long been considered the king of roasts. The prime rib is usually cut into boneless steaks by most producers. This is a shame, because prime rib is best on the bone, with a covering of its own natural fat. The bones provide a great depth of flavor, and work together with the fat to make the meat juicy and succulent. The herb garlic marinade in this recipe enhances and brings out the wonderful flavor of this true king of roasts.

Serves 4

2-rib prime rib roast, with fat cap (see note below)

For the Marinade

1 tablespoon fresh organic rosemary leaves

1 tablespoon fresh organic thyme leaves

1 tablespoon fresh organic Italian parsley leaves

4 cloves organic garlic, peeled

1 teaspoon freshly ground organic black pepper

3 tablespoons unfiltered organic extra virgin olive oil

For Roasting

1 teaspoon coarse unrefined sea salt, crushed

1. The day before you plan to cook the roast, make the marinade. Place the fresh herbs and garlic on a cutting board, and chop together until they are all finely chopped, and well combined. Mix the chopped herbs and garlic with the black pepper and the olive oil. Mix well. Rub the marinade over the meat sides of the roast. Let sit at room temperature for 1 hour, then cover and refrigerate overnight.

2. An hour before you plan to cook the roast, remove it from the refrigerator so it can come to room temperature.

3. Preheat the oven to 425 degrees. While the oven is preheating, scrape the marinade off the meat sides of the roast with a spoon, and reserve. Sprinkle the salt on all sides of the roast, including the bone side. Put the herb garlic marinade on top of the fat cap, pressing it into the fat.

4. When the oven has preheated, place the roast in the center of a large roasting pan, bone side down. Place the roast in the oven and cook for 20 minutes.

5. Reduce the heat to 300 degrees. Cook for 25 minutes.

6. Reduce the heat to 250 degrees. Cook for 10 minutes. Check for doneness. If the roast is not done to your taste, keep checking at 5 minute intervals.

Get ready to eat some of the most tender and delicious prime rib you have ever had.

NOTE: If the roast does not have a fat cap, cover with beef tallow, or thinly sliced pastured butter, or strips of good natural bacon.

Anointed Ribeye Roast with Roasted Potatoes

Ribeye, which is a boneless rib roast, is one of the most flavorful cuts of beef, especially when grassfed. This roast is even tastier than most, because it is "anointed" by having hot beef fat poured over it just before cooking. This flavorful hot basting seals and flavors the meat, making it even juicier and more tasty. The simple marinade prepares the meat for its anointment, resulting in a juicy, beefy roast. The roasted potatoes go perfectly with the meat. This is a dish to savor.

Serves 4

1 (2 pound) ribeye roast

For the Marinade
2 tablespoons unfiltered organic extra virgin olive oil

2 large organic garlic cloves, finely chopped

1 teaspoon freshly ground organic black pepper

For the Potatoes
4 tablespoons beef tallow or beef suet, cut into shavings or crumbled

Many, many potatoes

For the Roast
1 teaspoon coarse unrefined sea salt, crushed

4 more tablespoons of beef tallow or beef suet

1. The night before you plan to cook the roast, combine the olive oil, garlic, and pepper into a marinade. Coat the meat with the marinade, and place it in a covered glass bowl. Let it rest for 1 hour, and refrigerate overnight. (Alternatively, you could cook it the same day after marinating it for 1 hour.)

2. Remove the meat from the refrigerator about an hour before cooking, so it can come to room temperature.

3. Peel the potatoes and cut each potato into 3 to 6 circular pieces. Spread 4 tablespoons of the shaved or crumbled beef fat over the roasting pan. Place the roasting pan in the oven.

4. Preheat the oven to 425 degrees. Remove the pan from the preheating oven once the fat has melted.

5. Melt the remaining 4 tablespoons beef fat in a frying pan. Place the roast on a plate. Sprinkle the roast with the salt. Carefully pour the melted beef fat from the frying pan over the roast. Try to pour some fat over the sides of the roast, as well as the top. Using tongs, carefully place the anointed roast in the center of the roasting pan, fat side up. Surround the roast with the potatoes. Place the roast in the preheated oven.

6. Cook for 10 minutes, then remove the pan from the oven. Baste the roast, and turn over the potatoes.

7. Cook for another 10 minutes, then remove the pan from the oven. Baste the roast, and turn over the potatoes.

8. Turn the heat down to 300 degrees. Return the pan to the oven, and cook for another 15 minutes for rare, (or cook for another 20 minutes for medium rare). If the meat is not done to your taste, continue to cook at 300 degrees, testing for doneness every 5 minutes.

Remove the roast from the oven, and let the meat rest in a warm place while you gather up the magnificent, crusty potatoes. The combination of the juicy meat with the crusty, soft on the inside, melt in your mouth potatoes is sublime.

Ribeye Roasted in the English Style
on a Bed of Garlic

While a bone in prime rib may be the ultimate roast, boneless ribeye is also terrific. The English custom of roasting at relatively high heat is usually used for a bone in roast, but works very well here. Garlic and onion are not English, but using a bed of garlic and onion to replace the bones gives fantastic flavor to the meat. The garlic becomes soft, sweet and nutty from being roasted under a prime rib, and makes a great garnish. This one is juicy and tender, with a deep beefy flavor.

Serves 4 to 6

1 (2 to 3 pound) ribeye roast, with fat cap (see note below)

For the Marinade
2 tablespoons unfiltered organic extra virgin olive oil

For Roasting
1 tablespoon organic extra virgin olive oil
1 bulb organic garlic
1 medium organic onion, cut into three circles of equal thickness
½ teaspoon coarse unrefined natural sea salt, crushed

1. The night before you plan to cook the roast, rub with the unfiltered olive oil. Let sit at room temperature for 1 hour, then place in a glass bowl, cover, and refrigerate. (Alternatively, you could cook it the same day after marinating it for 1 hour.)

2. At least 1 hour before you plan to cook the roast, take it out of the refrigerator so it can come to room temperature.

3. Break the garlic bulbs into individual cloves. Discard the loose skins, but do not peel the cloves. Place in a small bowl, and coat with the olive oil.

4. Preheat the oven to 425 degrees. In the center of a greased roasting pan, use the onion circles and the garlic cloves to make a bed slightly larger than the roast.

5. When the oven is preheated, sprinkle the meat with the salt. Place the roast on the bed of vegetables, and put the pan in the center of the oven. Roast for 30 minutes, and check for doneness. If the roast is not done, check for doneness at 5 minute intervals. It should be done in 30 to 45 minutes, depending on the size of the roast and the degree of doneness you prefer.

Serve with the caramelized garlic and onions. Remove the skin from the garlic before eating.

NOTE: If the roast does not have a fat cap, cover with beef tallow, or thinly sliced pastured butter, or strips of good natural bacon.

Strip Loin Roast

The strip loin, also known as New York steak, has some of the most delicious and tender meat, when properly cooked. It has a deep, juicy, beefy flavor. Before the twentieth century, this cut of meat was usually called "sirloin." The very fact that the word consisted of the words "Sir" and "Loin"showed the high regard the English had for this magnificent cut of beef. It is the only cut of beef to be addressed as noble. This is one of the more expensive cuts, and is usually cut into steaks. It's luxurious as a roast, and the English loved to roast it. This recipe is designed to bring out the wonderful natural flavor of this noble roast.

Serves 4

1 (2 pound) strip loin roast, with fat cap

For the Marinade

2 tablespoons unfiltered organic extra virgin olive oil

For Roasting

1 medium organic onion, peeled and cut into 3 circles of equal thickness

1 teaspoon coarse unrefined sea salt, crushed

½ teaspoon freshly ground organic black pepper

1. At least 2 hours before you plan to cook the roast, rub the olive oil into the meat. Let sit at room temperature for at least 2 hours.

2. Preheat the oven to 425 degrees.

3. Place the onion circles close together in a roasting pan to make a bed for the roast. Sprinkle the salt and pepper over the meat. Place the meat on the onions, fat side up.

4. Put the roast in the oven. Cook for 12 minutes if you want it rare, or 15 minutes if you want it medium to medium rare.

5. Remove the roast from the oven, baste with the pan drippings, and return to the oven for another 12 or 15 minutes, depending on how you want it done.

Serve and enjoy.

Beef Wellington

This is a famous old dish that can be absolutely superb, if done well. It was named for the Duke of Wellington, England's greatest general, who loved to eat. The combination of a tenderloin baked in a puff pastry crust, smothered in sautéed mushrooms and onions — is scrumptious. While some versions cover the meat with foie gras, I have always preferred to use a combination of mushrooms and onions, finely chopped, sautéed in butter and truffle oil. When my wife asked me to make Beef Wellington for her birthday after we switched to grassfed beef, I had a moment of doubt. Since grassfed meat cooks so much faster, how could I cook the meat to a perfect medium rare AND make sure the crust was properly cooked?

The solution was simple. This is the only time in the book where I do not bring the meat to room temperature before cooking. I reasoned that since the tenderloin was pre-browned, and cooked in a crust, the meat would be tender even if it was cold when the cooking started. It worked! Both the meat and the crust came out great. This is a superb dish for a special occasion.

Serves 4

    1 (2 pound) tenderloin roast, trimmed of all sinew and connective tissue

    1 package natural puff pastry, (made with real butter only)

For Pre-Browning

    2 tablespoons pastured butter

For the Mushroom Coating

    1 pound crimini or fresh shiitake mushrooms, finely chopped

    1 medium organic onion, finely chopped

    2 tablespoons black truffle oil, (or 2 tablespoons extra virgin olive oil)

    2 tablespoons pastured butter

    1 large organic egg, beaten with a fork

For the Final Roasting

    1 organic egg yolk, beaten with a fork

1. The day before you plan to make Beef Wellington, heat 2 tablespoons of pastured butter over medium heat in a cast iron frying pan. When the butter is hot and slightly smoking, brown the roast on all sides over medium heat. Let rest on a plate for 1 hour, then place in a glass bowl, cover, and refrigerate overnight.

2. About 1 hour before you plan to cook the Beef Wellington, make the mushroom coating. (Remember to refrigerate the meat until Step 4.) Mix the onions and mushrooms together in a bowl. Melt the butter over medium heat in a large frying pan. Add the truffle oil. When the oil and butter are hot, dump the onion and mushroom mixture into the frying pan. Turn the heat to high, and stir the mixture for about 5 minutes, or until the mushrooms have really cooked down and have started to brown. Remove the mixture from the pan, place in a bowl, and let cool for at least 30 minutes. When the mixture is cool, or just slightly warm, stir in the beaten egg, and mix well.

3. Grease a large roasting pan. Place half of the puff pastry on the roasting pan. Coat the sheet with half of the onion mushroom mixture.

4. Take the meat out of the refrigerator, and place it on the coated pastry sheet. Coat the meat with the other half of the mixture. Use the rest of the puff pastry to cover the roast, pressing the edges of the two pastry sheets together so they close and completely cover the meat. Brush the top and sides of the pastry with the egg yolk. Use a fork to make numerous small holes over the top and sides of the pastry.

5. Preheat the oven to 450 degrees.

6. Place the roast in the oven, and cook for 15 minutes.

7. Turn the heat down to 350 degrees, and cook for another 15 minutes.

Slice and serve this most excellent dish. Fit for a duke!

Strip Loin Roast with Double Herb Crust

The short loin is one of the most flavorful and tender cuts of beef. It also has many names, which can be confusing. This wonderful cut of beef is known as New York steak (but not in New York), Kansas City steak, strip steak, Delmonico steak, strip loin, and before the 20th century it was called sirloin. Whatever you call it, it is one of the most prized cuts of beef, appreciated for its robust flavor and tenderness. We'll call it strip loin. Strip loin is usually cut into steaks, and makes a very fine steak indeed. Strip loin also makes one of the best roasts you will ever have. It usually has a fat cap, which adds to its flavor and tenderness.

Cooking roasts in an herb crust is traditional in Europe. The herbs go really well with this roast, enhancing and deepening its flavor. Traditional recipes use either dried or fresh herbs, never both. We use both fresh and dried herbs in this recipe, which is why we call it "double." Using both together more than doubles the flavor.

Serves 4

1 (2 pound) strip loin roast, with fat cap

For the Marinade

2 tablespoons unfiltered organic extra virgin olive oil

1 tablespoon fresh organic rosemary leaves, finely chopped

1 tablespoon fresh thyme leaves, finely chopped

1 teaspoon organic dried rosemary leaves, crushed

1 teaspoon dried thyme leaves, crushed

1 teaspoon freshly ground organic black pepper

For Roasting

1 teaspoon coarse unrefined sea salt, crushed

1 organic onion, cut into three circles of equal thickness

1. The night before you plan to cook the roast, mix all the marinade ingredients together. Rub the marinade all over the roast. Place it in a covered glass bowl. Let it sit at room temperature for 1 hour, then refrigerate overnight.

2. An hour before you plan to cook the roast, take it out of the refrigerator so it can come to room temperature.

3. Preheat the oven to 425 degrees. Sprinkle the roast with the salt. Place the onions close together in a roasting pan, then place the roast on the onion circles. Cook for 15 minutes.

4. Baste the roast with the pan drippings. Turn the oven down to 250 degrees, and cook for another 15 to 30 minutes, depending on how you like it.

Serve and enjoy.

Roast Sirloin

Sirloin roasts have a distinct taste and texture, and are absolutely delicious. The meat has a deep beefy flavor that is quite different from prime rib, and quite excellent. The meat is tender, and has a slight sweetness to it. The use of the onions as a roasting rack really helps set off the flavor of this wonderful roast, and the *Secret Seasoning Salt* brings out every last bit of its great natural flavor. This one is good, really good.

Serves 4 to 6

1 (2 to 2½ pound) top sirloin roast with fat cap (see note below)

For the Marinade
2 tablespoons unfiltered organic extra virgin olive oil

For Roasting
1 medium organic onion, cut into 3 thick circles of roughly equal size
2 teaspoons *Secret Seasoning Salt* (page 186), crushed

1. The night before you plan to cook the meat, rub it on all sides with the unfiltered olive oil. Place in a glass bowl, cover, and let rest at room temperature for 1 hour, then refrigerate overnight.

2. At least 1 hour before you plan to cook the roast, take it out of the refrigerator so it can come to room temperature.

3. Preheat the oven to 425 degrees. Grease a roasting pan, and arrange the onion circles close together to form a rack for the roast. Rub the *Secret Seasoning Salt* all over the roast. Place the roast on the onion circles, and put the pan in the center of the oven. Cook at 425 degrees for 10 minutes.

4. Remove the roast from the oven, and baste it with the pan drippings. Return the roast to the oven, and cook for another 10 minutes.

5. Remove the roast from the oven, and baste it with the pan drippings. Turn the heat down to 250 degrees. Return to the oven, and cook for 30 minutes.

6. Test for doneness. If the roast is not done, return to the oven, and check for doneness at 5 minute intervals.

Serve, and enjoy the time honored taste of a great sirloin roast.

NOTE: If the roast does not have a fat cap, cover with beef tallow, or thinly sliced pastured butter, or strips of good natural bacon.

High-Low Roast Beef

One of the most traditional ways to roast meat was to build a hot fire, burn it down to coals, and put the meat on a spit in front of the fire. The cooking temperature was very hot at first. The temperature gradually reduced as the fire burned down. The meat was basted regularly, usually with melted animal fat. By the time the meat was ready, the fire had gone from a high heat to a very low one.

This ancient cooking technique is quite different from more modern techniques which call for cooking the meat at an even temperature.

Since the meat that was originally cooked by this technique was all grassfed, I decided to recreate this method in an oven to see how much the ancients knew about cooking meat. It turns out that the ancients knew a lot. The results were so outstanding in terms of taste and tenderness, that I had to preserve the recipe. Here it is:

Serves 4 to 6

1 (2 to 3 pound) sirloin tip roast, (or center cut shoulder)

For the Marinade
2 tablespoons unfiltered organic extra virgin olive oil

For Roasting
1 medium organic onion, peeled and cut into 4 circles of equal thickness
1 teaspoon coarse unrefined sea salt, crushed
1 tablespoon pastured butter, sliced thin
2 tablespoons beef suet, (or beef lard), in small pieces

1. Two hours before you plan to start cooking the meat, take it out of the refrigerator, and rub the olive oil all over the meat. Use enough oil to coat the entire roast. Let it rest for 2 hours at room temperature.

2. Preheat oven to 425 degrees, with the rack in the middle of the oven. Place the onion circles together in the middle of a roasting pan. Rub the salt all over the meat. Place the meat on the onions. Cover the top of the meat with thinly sliced butter and the small pieces of beef suet (or lard).

3. Put the pan in the oven, and cook for 15 minutes.

4. Remove the pan from the oven. Baste the roast generously with the melted fat. Then return to the oven. Cook for another 15 minutes.

5. Remove the pan from the oven, and baste the roast generously. Put the roast back in the oven, close the oven, and turn the oven off.

6. Remove the roast from the oven after 15 minutes, and check the temperature of the roast with a meat thermometer. Continue checking at 10 minute intervals until the roast is done to your liking.

Serve and enjoy.

Roast Sirloin Tip with Apple Onion Marinade

This may sound unusual, and it is. Unusually delicious. The enzymes in the apple make the meat quite tender, and the flavor is exquisite. It is very important to use an organic apple, not apple juice. Apple juice will not work because the pasteurization process destroys the very enzymes that are needed to tenderize the meat. The green onions and the garlic balance the apple perfectly, creating a wonderful flavor. Roasting the beef on top of the very apples used to marinate it also enhances the flavor, and creates deeply flavored drippings that are a great base for any gravy.

Serves 4

1 (2 pound) sirloin tip roast, (or any tender roast), with fat cap (see note below)

For the Marinade

1 organic fuji apple, peeled, sliced, and crushed
2 organic green onions, coarsely chopped and crushed
2 organic garlic cloves, crushed

For Roasting

1 teaspoon coarse unrefined sea salt, crushed

1. Combine the apples, green onions, and garlic. Mix well. Press this mixture into all sides of the meat. Marinate at room temperature for 2 hours, or refrigerate overnight in a covered glass bowl.

2. If you have refrigerated the meat, take it out at least 1 hour before you plan to cook it, so it can come to room temperature.

3. Preheat the oven to 425 degrees. Scrape the marinade off the meat. Use the marinade to make a bed in the center of the roasting pan in the approximate shape of the roast. Sprinkle the meat with the salt.

4. Place the roast in the preheated oven, and roast for 10 minutes.

5. Baste the roast with the drippings, and return to the oven. Roast for another 10 minutes.

6. Baste the roast with the drippings, and return to the oven. Reduce the heat to 250 degrees. Roast for 20 minutes.

Serve and enjoy. Be sure to serve the caramelized vegetables from the pan.

NOTE: If the roast does not have a fat cap, cover with beef tallow, or thinly sliced pastured butter, or strips of good natural bacon.

Super Tender Roast Beef

Some people find it hard to believe that grassfed beef can be tender enough to cut with a fork. They haven't tried this recipe. This is a combination of traditional Polish and German methods of cooking beef. No knife is needed.

Serves 6

1 (3 pound) center cut shoulder roast, (also known as center cut cross rib)

For Pre-Browning
2 tablespoons pastured butter

For Roasting
1 small onion, sliced into 4 circles of equal thickness
Coarse unrefined sea salt, crushed
Freshly ground organic black pepper
2 tablespoons beef tallow
1 tablespoon pastured butter

1. Melt 2 tablespoons of butter in a cast iron frying pan over medium heat. When the butter is hot, bubbly, and slightly smoking, carefully brown the roast on all sides. Do not leave it on any one side for too long, as the goal is to brown it, not scorch it. It's important that the roast is thoroughly browned all over. Never raise the heat above medium.

2. There are two alternate ways of doing the next step, which is crucial. The first is to let the roast cool in a glass bowl for about 1 hour, cover, and refrigerate overnight. Or, you can let it rest at room temperature approximately 2 hours.

3. If you have refrigerated the meat, take it out at least 1 hour before you plan to cook it, so it can come to room temperature.

4. Preheat the oven to 425 degrees. Place the 4 onion circles in a square formation (2 rows of 2 circles) in a roasting pan. Season the meat lightly with salt and pepper. Place the roast on the onion circles. Cut 2 tablespoons of beef tallow into shavings, and place them on top of the roast. Place 1 tablespoon of butter on top of the roast.

5. Put the pan in the preheated oven, and cook for 10 minutes.

6. Remove the pan from the oven, and baste the roast with melted fat in the pan. Reduce the heat to 250 degrees, put the pan in the oven, and roast for 40 minutes. Check for doneness. If it is not done to your taste, return it to the oven, and check at 5 minute intervals.

You will have an exceptionally tender and flavorful roast.

High-Low Roast Beef on a Vegetable Rack

Most beef roasts today are boneless. I suppose it makes shipping easier, but the bones make a great natural rack. Many cooking authorities advocate roasting boneless roasts on some kind of metal rack. I've never liked this, and used to put the roast directly on the roasting pan. The bottom of the roast usually ended up scorched, which I also didn't like. Once again, tradition came to the rescue. Several Baltic peoples traditionally put various vegetables under a boneless roast. The vegetables not only keep the bottom of the roast from scorching, but they caramelize throughout the roasting process, and create a wonderful aroma and flavor throughout the meat. Carrots and onions are used in Estonia. I've added some garlic. This roast is nothing short of wonderful.

Serves 6 to 8

1 (3 to 4 pound) center cut shoulder roast, (or sirloin tip), with fat cap (see note below)

For the Marinade
2 tablespoons unfiltered organic extra virgin olive oil

For Roasting
2 organic carrots, peeled and cut into 4 inch long pieces

1 medium onion, sliced into 4 circles of equal thickness

4 whole organic garlic cloves, washed but unpeeled

1 teaspoon coarse unrefined sea salt, crushed

1. The day before you plan to cook the roast, rub the olive oil all over the meat, coating it evenly. Place the meat in a covered glass bowl. Let rest at room temperature for 1 hour, then refrigerate overnight.

2. Remove the meat from the refrigerator at least 1 hour before you plan to cook the meat, so it can come to room temperature.

3. Preheat the oven to 425 degrees. While the oven is preheating, grease the roasting pan thoroughly with butter or olive oil. Arrange the vegetables in the roasting pan to make a bed for the roast. This may take some tinkering, but group the vegetables together in such a way that when you place the roast on the vegetables, they will keep the roast from touching the pan.

4. When the oven has preheated, rub the salt into the meat sides of the roast. Place the roast on the vegetables. Put the pan in the preheated oven. Cook for 20 minutes.

5. Turn the oven down to 300 degrees. Cook for another 20 minutes.

6. Turn the oven down to 250 degrees. Cook for 15 minutes. Test for doneness. If not done to your taste, continue testing at 10 minute intervals.

Serve and enjoy the deep, satisfying taste of the meat. The caramelized vegetables in the rack are also quite tasty.

NOTE: If the roast does not have a fat cap, cover with beef tallow, or thinly sliced pastured butter, or strips of good natural bacon.

Twice Cooked Roast Beef with German Roasting Vegetables

This delicious recipe highlights another cooking technique that results in tender grassfed beef. Browning the roast in wonderful pastured butter, with a long resting period, results in meat with a deep beefy flavor that is marvelously tender. No marinade is needed. In the final roasting, the roast picks up great flavor when it is cooked on a bed of traditional roasting vegetables. Traditional vegetable combinations become traditions for a reason — they taste great.

While this technique may seem unusual, give it a try. You'll be happy you did.

Serves 4

1 (2 to 3 pound) center cut shoulder roast, (or sirloin tip), with fat cap

For Pre-Browning
2 tablespoons pastured butter

For Roasting
½ **teaspoon coarse unrefined sea salt, crushed**

½ **teaspoon freshly ground organic black pepper**

½ **teaspoon organic onion powder**

1 medium organic onion, chopped

1 organic carrot, peeled and cut into small slices

1 organic leek, chopped

4 sprigs fresh flat leaf parsley, with stems, chopped

4 sprigs fresh organic thyme, chopped

2 tablespoons pastured butter, thinly sliced

1. The night before you plan to cook the roast (or at least 8 hours before), place the butter in a cast iron frying pan over medium heat. Dry the meat thoroughly. When the butter is hot and slightly smoking, brown the roast on all sides over medium heat. This should take 8 to 10 minutes, depending on the shape of the roast. It is important that all surfaces be browned. The meat should range from golden brown to deep brown, but should not be scorched.

2. When the meat is browned, remove from the pan, and let rest on a plate for 1 hour. It is important that the meat cool down before you put it in the refrigerator, to prevent it from being steamed when covered. Place the meat in a glass or ceramic bowl, cover, and refrigerate.

3. An hour before you plan to cook the roast, remove it from the refrigerator so it can come to room temperature.

4. Preheat the oven to 425 degrees. Mix the salt, pepper, and onion powder and rub them all over the roast. Place all the vegetables in the center of a greased roasting pan. Push them into a bed that is just a little bit larger than the shape of your roast. Place the roast right on top of the vegetables, fat side up. Use the butter slices to cover that portion of the top of the roast that is not covered by the fat cap. Put the roast in the oven, and cook for 15 minutes.

5. Remove the roast from the oven, and baste with the pan drippings. Turn the oven down to 300 degrees, return the roast to the oven, and cook for another 15 minutes.

6. Check for doneness. If the roast is not done, turn the heat down to 250 degrees, and check for doneness at 5 minute intervals. Please bear in mind that a roast that has been pre-browned like this will cook faster than usual.

Serve and enjoy the deep, rich flavors. The pan vegetables make a delicious garnish.

Traditional European Roast with Triple Onion and Triple Garlic

A surprising number of older European roast recipes call for rubbing beef with olive oil. These are older recipes, so the olive oil would have to have been unfiltered and organic, since there was nothing else at that time. Some of the recipes from Northern Europe suggested covering the olive oil coated meat with sliced onions, and letting it marinate prior to cooking. Some of the recipes from Southern Europe were similar, but used sliced garlic instead. Since I love the taste of onions and garlic with beef, I decided to use both. I also decided to intensify the flavor by sprinkling the meat with powdered onion and powdered garlic. Finally, the meat receives a third blast of onion-garlic flavoring when it is cooked over a bed of onions and garlic, which provide yet a third nuance of onion-garlic flavor as they roast under the meat. The combination of fresh and dried onions and garlic enhances the great natural flavor of grassfed beef, and creates a combination of flavors that is much more than the sum of its parts. This one's a winner.

Serves 4 to 6

1 (2 to 3 pound) center cut shoulder roast, (or sirloin tip), with fat cap (see note below)

For the Marinade

2 tablespoons unfiltered organic extra virgin olive oil

Organic onion powder

Organic granulated garlic powder

1 large organic onion, sliced

4 large garlic cloves, finely chopped

1. The day before you plan to cook the roast, rub the olive oil into the meat. Sprinkle evenly with onion powder and granulated garlic, being sure to coat every side of the meat lightly, but evenly. Put the meat in a marinating bowl. Cover the meat with the onions and garlic, making sure that all sides of the meat are in contact with some of the vegetables. Refrigerate overnight in a covered glass bowl.

2. Take the meat out of the refrigerator at least 1 hour before you plan to cook it, so it can come to room temperature.

3. Preheat the oven to 425 degrees. While the oven is heating, grease a small roasting pan. Remove the meat from the marinade, and place the garlic and onions in the center of the roasting pan. Push them into a bed that is just a little bit larger than the shape of your roast. Place the roast right on top of the vegetables, fat side up.

4. Place the pan in a preheated oven. Cook for 15 minutes.

5. Remove the roast from the oven, baste with the pan drippings, return to the oven, and cook for another 15 minutes.

6. Check for doneness. If the roast is not done, turn off the oven. Return the roast to the turned off oven, and check for doneness at 10 minute intervals.

Serve and enjoy. Try some of the caramelized vegetables, they are delicious.

NOTE: If the roast does not have a fat cap, cover with beef tallow, or thinly sliced pastured butter, or strips of good natural bacon.

Roast Beef with Thyme Garlic Pepper Rub
on a Bed of Leeks

It is astonishing how just a few carefully chosen herbs and spices can really transform and intensify the taste of a great piece of meat. Thyme is another herb that really enhances the great natural flavor of grassfed beef without overwhelming it. Thyme has been used all over Europe to flavor meat. We combine it with garlic and pepper for yet another classic flavor combination. Leeks are a favorite in Wales and Germany, and they really work well with the thyme-garlic combination, enhancing the flavor. You could use green onions or onions instead of leeks, but leeks work perfectly in this recipe. Once again, the unfiltered extra virgin olive oil carries the flavor of the herbs right into the meat, and the results are sublime.

Serves 4 to 5

1 (2 to 2½) pound center cut shoulder roast, (or sirloin tip), with fat cap (see note below)

For the Marinade

12 organic thyme sprigs

2 cloves organic garlic, chopped

½ teaspoon freshly ground organic black pepper

2 tablespoons unfiltered organic extra virgin olive oil

For Roasting

1 organic leek, including the green leaves, cleaned, halved lengthwise, and cut into 3 inch lengths

½ teaspoon coarse unrefined sea salt, crushed

1. The day before you plan to cook the roast, make the marinade. Strip the thyme leaves from the stems, and chop them finely. Reserve the stems. Combine the leaves with the garlic, pepper, and olive oil to make the marinade. Rub the marinade all over the meat. Place the roast is a glass bowl, let rest for 1 hour, then cover and refrigerate overnight.

2. Take the meat out of the refrigerator about 1 hour before you plan to cook it, so it can come to room temperature.

3. Preheat the oven to 425 degrees. Make a bed of the leeks and thyme stems. Sprinkle the roast with salt. Place the roast on the bed. Cook for 10 minutes.

4. Baste with the pan drippings, and roast for another 10 minutes.

5. Turn the heat down to 250 degrees, and roast for another 20 minutes. Check for doneness. If not done to your taste, return to the oven, and check for doneness at 5 minute intervals.

Serve and enjoy.

NOTE: If the roast does not have a fat cap, cover with beef tallow, or thinly sliced pastured butter, or strips of good natural bacon.

Rosemary Pepper Roast on a Bed of Garlic

Grassfed beef has a wonderful natural flavor. Just a few of the right spices can really bring out and enhance that great natural flavor.

What are the right spices? Every cuisine has traditional flavor combinations, which have stood the test of time. Rosemary has been used to flavor meat all over Europe. Black pepper has been used all over the world to flavor beef, as has garlic. When you combine the three, you have a combination that is much more than the sum of its parts. The combination of rosemary, black pepper, and garlic is a favorite in Tuscany. When you use organic fresh rosemary, organic black pepper, and organic fresh garlic, and add some olive oil to carry the flavors into the meat, it's even better. This roast is just delicious.

Serves 4 to 6

1 (2 to 3 pound) center cut shoulder roast, (or sirloin tip, or top sirloin), with fat cap (see note below)

For the Marinade

2 tablespoons unfiltered organic extra virgin olive oil

Leaves from 2 sprigs of fresh organic rosemary, finely chopped

Freshly ground organic black pepper

For Roasting

1 bulb fresh organic garlic, broken into individual cloves, but left unpeeled

1 teaspoon coarse unrefined sea salt, crushed

1. The day before you plan to cook the roast, coat it with the olive oil. Press the chopped rosemary leaves into all sides of the meat. Sprinkle the pepper on all sides of the meat, and press it in. Let the meat rest in a glass bowl for 1 hour, then cover and refrigerate overnight.

2. An hour before you plan to cook the roast, take the roast out of the refrigerator so it can come to room temperature.

3. Preheat the oven to 425 degrees. Place the garlic cloves in the center of a lightly greased roasting pan, so they can form a bed for the roast. Once the oven has preheated, sprinkle the salt over the roast. Place the roast on the garlic cloves.

4. Put the roast in the oven, and cook for 10 minutes. Baste the roast, then cook for another 10 minutes.

5. Turn the heat down to 250 degrees, and cook for 20 to 30 minutes, until done to your taste.

Serve, and enjoy the wonderful classic flavors.

NOTE: If the roast does not have a fat cap, cover with beef tallow, or thinly sliced pastured butter, or strips of good natural bacon.

Romanian Roast Beef

Romania is an ancient land. The Romanians admired their ancient conquerors, the Romans, so much that they named themselves after them. They happily adopted the Roman obsession with food, but developed their own cuisine, which is both original and delicious. Romanian food is bold, hearty, and full of flavor. Beef is a favorite, and this recipe is based on a very traditional Romanian dish. Even though the traditional dish did not call for a marinade, I've discovered that this marinade intensifies the flavor, while making the meat more tender. The use of bacon and butter together is unusual, but gives an absolutely delicious result. You don't need a fat cap for this roast.

Serves 4 to 6

1 (2 to 3 pound) center cut shoulder roast, (or sirloin tip), no fat cap needed

For the Marinade
    4 large leafy sprigs organic Italian parsley, with stems
    4 large cloves organic garlic, skins removed
    1 large organic onion, sliced
    ½ teaspoon freshly ground organic black pepper
    2 tablespoons unfiltered organic extra virgin olive oil

For Roasting
    Fat, traditionally made bacon to cover the roast
    2 tablespoons pastured butter

1. The night before you plan to cook the roast, prepare the marinade. Finely chop the garlic and parsley together. Add the pepper and olive oil, and mix well. Place the roast in a glass bowl. Rub the marinade all over the roast. Press the sliced onion into all sides of the roast. Let sit at room temperature for 1 hour, then cover and refrigerate overnight.

2. An hour before you plan to cook the roast, remove it from the refrigerator so it can come to room temperature. Scrape the marinade off the roast with a spoon, and reserve. (It's okay if some of the marinade stays on the meat.)

3. Preheat the oven to 425 degrees. Place the reserved marinade (which will be mostly vegetables) in the center of a lightly greased roasting pan. Push the vegetables into a bed that is just a little bit larger than the shape of your roast. Bury 2 tablespoons of butter in the marinade/vegetable bed. Place the roast on top of the marinade/vegetable bed, and cover the top of the roast with the bacon. Cook for 10 minutes at 425 degrees.

4. Remove the roast from the oven, baste with the pan drippings, and return to the oven. Cook for 10 more minutes at 425 degrees.

5. Remove the roast from the oven, baste with the pan drippings, and return to the oven. Turn the heat down to 250 degrees, and cook for another 20 minutes. Test for doneness. If the roast is not done, return to the oven, and check for doneness at 5 minute intervals.

Serve and enjoy this delightful taste of Romania.

Marinated Roast Beef with the Flavors of Spain

Spain has one of the most superb cuisines on the planet. This cuisine uses the excellence of natural ingredients, enhanced by the precise use of specific spices to come up with some of the best dishes that have ever been eaten. Fortunately, Spain exports many oils and spices of superb quality.

Pork, veal, and lamb are far more important in Spanish cuisine than beef, probably because of the tradition of slaughtering most calves, rather than trying to feed them through the winter. The ingredients in this marinade are traditionally used for pork, but they give a great flavor to this beef roast. The simple combination of garlic, paprika, and olive oil is far more than the sum of its parts. Try to use Spanish ingredients if you can. It really makes a difference.

Serves 4 to 6

> 1 (2 to 3 pound) center cut shoulder roast, (or sirloin tip), with fat cap (see note below)

For the Marinade

> 4 organic garlic cloves, finely chopped
>
> 1 teaspoon sweet paprika, preferably Spanish
>
> ¼ teaspoon hot paprika, preferably Spanish
>
> 2 tablespoons unfiltered organic extra virgin olive oil, preferably Spanish, such as Nùñez de Prado

For Roasting

> 1 medium organic onion, cut into 3 circles of equal thickness

1. At least 1 day before you plan to cook the roast, make the marinade. Mix the garlic, paprikas, and oil together in a bowl. Rub this red mixture all over the roast. Place the roast in a tight fitting glass bowl, let rest at room temperature for 1 hour. Cover and refrigerate overnight, or preferably for 2 to 3 nights.

2. Remove the roast from the refrigerator 1 hour before you plan to cook it, so it can come to room temperature.

3. Preheat the oven to 425 degrees. Place the onion circles together in the middle of a lightly greased roasting pan. Place the roast on the onion slices. Cook at 425 degrees for 10 minutes.

4. Remove the roast from the oven, baste with the pan drippings, and cook for 10 minutes more.

5. Remove the roast from the oven, baste with the pan drippings, and return to the oven. Turn the heat down to 250 degrees. Cook for 20 minutes. Test for doneness. If the roast is not done, return to the oven, and check for doneness at 5 minute intervals.

Serve and enjoy the superb flavor of Spain.

NOTE: If the roast does not have a fat cap, cover with beef tallow, or thinly sliced pastured butter, or strips of good natural bacon.

Spanish Style Pan Roast

You can make a delicious roast in an iron pot. In this case, a cast iron casserole acts like a stovetop oven, first, deliciously browning the beef, then serving as an oven as the beef is cooked at a consistently diminishing heat. The results are crusty, juicy, very tender, and utterly delicious. And very, very garlicky. This recipe was inspired by some Spanish techniques for cooking a thick piece of meat.

I define a pan roast as a roast that is cooked in a cast iron frying pan, with flavorings that have been used for pot roasts and stews. The difference is that a pan roast is cooked for a very short time, and should be rare or medium rare in the middle, while being beautifully browned on the outside.

Serves 4

1 center cut shoulder roast, about 3 inches thick, no fat cap needed

For the Marinade

2 tablespoons unfiltered organic extra virgin olive oil

8 cloves organic garlic, peeled, crushed, and chopped

1 teaspoon freshly ground organic black pepper

For Pan Roasting

1 teaspoon coarse unrefined sea salt, crushed

2 tablespoons pastured butter

1 tablespoon extra virgin olive oil, preferably Spanish

1. Rub the unfiltered olive oil all over the meat. Press the crushed garlic into all sides of the meat. Sprinkle the pepper over all sides of the meat. Place in a glass bowl, cover, and let rest for at least 2 hours at room temperature. (Or let rest for 1 hour at room temperature, and refrigerate overnight.)

2. If you refrigerated the meat, take it out of the refrigerator at least 1 hour before you plan to cook it, so it can come to room temperature.

3. Scrape the garlic off the meat and discard. Sprinkle the salt over all sides of the meat. Heat the butter and olive oil over medium heat in a cast iron casserole that is large enough to hold the roast. When the butter and olive oil are hot and slightly smoking, put the roast in the casserole. Cook at medium for 7½ minutes. Turn the roast over and cook for another 7½ minutes.

4. Turn the roast over, reduce the heat to low, cover the casserole, and cook for 5 minutes on each side.

5. Turn the heat off, and let the roast stay in the covered casserole for 10 minutes.

Serve, and enjoy one of the most delicious roasts you will ever eat. It should be rare in the middle, medium rare as you get closer to the top and bottom, and pink just before you reach the beautiful brown crust on the exterior. Delicious all the way through.

Friar Tuck's Pan Roast

When I was a small boy in the 1950s, one of the first books I read concerned the adventures of a certain Robin Hood. The only thing I remember from the book was a description of a meal eaten by Friar Tuck, a beef stew flavored with copious amounts of mushrooms and onions. The description was so vivid, that the thought of it makes me hungry to this day. The combination of sautéed mushrooms and onions has been used to flavor several traditional English dishes, such as Beef Wellington. Using some truffle oil to sauté the mushrooms carries the flavor to the next level.

I have used this time honored flavoring combination to enhance a pan roast of grassfed beef. This pan roast fulfilled my dreams of Friar Tuck's dish more than anything I've ever eaten.

Serves 4

For the Initial Browning

1 (2 to 3 pound) center cut shoulder roast, cut 2½ to 3½ inches thick, (or top sirloin roast)

2 tablespoons pastured butter

For the Mushrooms

1 pound crimini mushrooms, sliced, (or any good mushrooms other than supermarket white)

2 tablespoons pastured butter

2 tablespoons truffle oil, (or extra virgin olive oil)[1]

For the Onion

1 large organic onion, sliced

2 tablespoons pastured butter

For Pan Roasting

2 tablespoons pastured butter

½ teaspoon coarse unrefined sea salt, crushed

---

1   The truffle oil will give a wonderful flavor to the mushrooms. The mushrooms will still be very good just with extra virgin olive oil.

1. Melt 2 tablespoons butter in a cast iron casserole over medium heat. When the butter is hot and slightly smoking, brown the roast on all sides. This should take 6 to 10 minutes, depending on the shape of the roast. The goal is to get it nicely browned, not scorched.

2. When the roast is browned, place it on a plate, and let rest for at least 2 hours at room temperature. (Or let rest for 1 hour at room temperature, place in a glass bowl, cover, and refrigerate overnight.)

3. If you refrigerated the meat, take it out of the refrigerator at least 1 hour before you plan to cook it, so it can come to room temperature.

4. Heat the butter and oil for the mushrooms in a cast iron casserole over medium high heat. When the mixture is hot and slightly smoking, pour in the mushrooms and cook, stirring constantly, until the mushrooms are well browned. This should take about 5 minutes, and the mushrooms will shrink considerably. Remove the mushrooms to a bowl.

5. Take the butter for the onions, and melt it in the same casserole over medium high heat. When the butter is hot and slightly smoking, put the onions in the casserole, and cook until soft and golden brown, which should take about 5 minutes. Remove the onions to the same bowl as the mushrooms. The mushrooms should have released some liquid into the bowl, this is to be expected.

6. Reduce the heat in the casserole to medium, and add the butter for pan roasting. Sprinkle the roast with salt. When the butter is hot and slightly smoking, cook the roast over medium heat for 4 minutes on each side, for a total of 8 minutes.

7. Remove the roast from the casserole, and reduce the heat to low. Cover the bottom of the casserole with about half of the mushroom/onion mixture. Place the roast in the casserole. Pour the rest of the mushroom/onion mixture over the roast. Cover the casserole, and cook on low for 5 minutes. Turn the roast over, and put some of the mushroom/onion mixture on top, using a spoon. Cover the casserole, and cook for another 5 minutes.

8. Turn off the heat, and let the roast stay in the covered casserole for 10 minutes.

Remove and serve. Friar Tuck will envy you.

Brigand's Pan Roast

Several Balkan and Eastern European countries have a category of dishes which have the word "brigand," "bandit," or "robber" in them. Whether it is Hungary, or Poland, or Greece, or Serbia, or Bulgaria, or Romania, the explanation is always the same — brigands have to be able to take off at a moment's notice — so the faster they can cook their food, the more likely they'll be able to eat it. Speed is life, to a brigand. Most of these dishes call for marinated meat. There are contemporary reports of various brigands having bags of marinating meat tied to their saddles. I prefer a refrigerator.

Some of these brigands must have been former cooks, because these dishes can be great. Of course, the only meat available to these brigands was grassfed, which is great for us. The speed with which **Brigand's Pan Roast** can be cooked is consistent with the insane pace of modern life. This pan roast is tender, flavorful, and quick to cook.

Serves 4

1 (2 to 3 pound) tri-tip roast, (or top sirloin)

For the Marinade
2 tablespoons unfiltered organic extra virgin olive oil
3 medium organic onions, sliced

For Pan Roasting
3 tablespoons pastured butter
1 teaspoon coarse unrefined sea salt, crushed
¼ cup good homemade broth, such as *Beef* or *Nomad's Broth* (pages 45 - 53)

1. The night before you plan to cook the roast, put it in a glass bowl, rub it on all sides with the unfiltered olive oil, and surround it completely with the onions. Let rest at room temperature for 1 hour, then cover and refrigerate overnight.

2. An hour before you plan to cook the roast, take it out of the refrigerator so it can come to room temperature.

3. Heat the butter in a large cast iron frying pan over medium heat. When the butter is hot and slightly smoking, remove the roast from the marinade, and rub all sides of the roast with salt. Put the roast in the frying pan, and brown it over medium heat for 5 minutes. Turn the roast over, and brown it over medium heat for another 5 minutes.

4. Put the roast on a plate to rest. Add the onions to the frying pan, and sauté for 10 minutes, stirring occasionally. Add another tablespoon of butter, if necessary.

5. Push the onions to either side of the pan, and return the roast to the pan. Pour the broth over the roast. Turn the heat down to medium low, and cook for 5 minutes.

6. Turn the roast over, baste with the pan juices, and cook for another 5 minutes.

Serve with the onions which should be sweet, caramelized, and wonderful.

Exotic Yankee Pot Roast

Yankee pot roast is a traditional American dish that goes back to Colonial times. Back then, all beef was grassfed. I suspect, like so many traditional recipes, that the other ingredients varied with what was available. It appears to have been made with beef or venison, and cooked in broth with one or more vegetables. This version is exotic, because it uses leeks, rather than the usual onions. The combination of ingredients here seems simple, but the flavor is deep and satisfying.

Serves 4 to 6

1 (3 pound) rump roast, (or chuck)

For Pre-Browning
2 tablespoons pastured butter

1 tablespoon organic extra virgin olive oil

For Pot Roasting
2 medium organic leeks, well cleaned, and chopped into small pieces

1 teaspoon coarse unrefined sea salt, crushed

1 teaspoon freshly ground organic black pepper

4 medium organic carrots, peeled, and roughly chopped

6 small organic russet potatoes, peeled and chopped into small pieces

1 to 2 cups of good homemade broth, such as *Beef* or *Nomad's Broth* (pages 45 - 53)

1 tablespoon arrowroot, mixed with 1 tablespoon filtered water

1. The proper browning of the roast is crucial to the success of this dish. In a cast iron casserole, heat the butter and the olive oil together over medium heat, until hot. Dry the roast, and brown all sides over medium heat. Be careful not to scorch the roast. Scorching should not happen if you use medium heat. Make sure you have enough butter and oil in the pot, and turn the roast regularly. When all sides of the roast are nicely browned, remove the roast to a plate, and let it rest while you peel and chop the vegetables.

2. Add the chopped leeks to the fat and drippings, and brown over medium heat for about 10 minutes, stirring occasionally to prevent scorching. This will caramelize the leeks, cause them to shrink in size, and bring out their flavor.

3. Sprinkle the roast all over with the salt and pepper. Put the roast in the pot with the leeks. Add the carrots and potatoes. Add enough broth to come halfway up the sides of the roast, making sure there's enough broth to cover the potatoes. Cover the casserole, and let it simmer slowly for about 1½ hours.

4. Test for doneness by sticking a big fork or skewer into the roast. If it goes in easily, the roast is ready. If it doesn't, the roast needs more simmering. Check for doneness at 15 minute intervals.

5. When the roast is ready, remove the meat from the pot and let it rest on a warm plate. Remove the potatoes from the pot with a slotted spoon, and place in a bowl. Bring the rest of the pot to a strong simmer, and add the arrowroot/water mixture. Simmer until the gravy thickens somewhat.

Hunter's Pot Roast

Many European countries have a type of dish that has the word "Hunter" somewhere in it. This usually means that the dish is made up of some meat that is flavored with juniper berries or mushrooms, or made with a marinade that is typically used to flavor and tenderize game. Unfortunately, all of these marinades contained a good amount of vinegar and/or wine, which can dry out grassfed meat. I decided to try a pot roast using those delicious flavors, but omitting the vinegar and wine.

This pot roast contains traditional flavors applied in a non-traditional way. The roast is not only well-flavored, but beautifully tender, without being mushy or dry.

Serves 4

1 (3 pound) chuck roast, (or rump)

For the Marinade

10 juniper berries, crushed

20 organic black peppercorns, crushed

½ teaspoon organic dried thyme, crushed

2 imported bay leaves, broken into small pieces and crushed

2 tablespoons unfiltered organic extra virgin olive oil

1 large organic onion, sliced

3 leafy stalks organic celery, from the center of the bunch, chopped

2 organic carrots, peeled and chopped

½ bunch organic Italian parsley, including the stems, chopped

For Pot Roasting

2 tablespoons pastured butter

1 to 2 cups of good homemade broth, such as *Nomad's Broth* (page 50)

1 teaspoon coarse unrefined sea salt, crushed

1 tablespoon arrowroot, mixed with 1 tablespoon filtered water

1. Combine the juniper berries, peppercorns, thyme, bay leaves, and olive oil. Rub this into the meat on all surfaces. Place the roast in a marinating bowl which is just large enough to hold it and all the vegetables. Mix the vegetables together, and add them to the bowl, making sure that the meat is surrounded on all sides by vegetables. Cover the bowl, and marinate for 1 hour at room temperature. (See note below.)

2. Refrigerate for at least 2 hours, preferably overnight.

3. An hour before you plan to cook the roast, remove the roast from the refrigerator so it can come to room temperature.

4. Remove the roast from the marinade, brushing off any vegetables that cling to the meat. Reserve the vegetables. Melt the butter in a cast iron casserole over medium heat, until hot and slightly smoking. Brown the roast on all sides. The goal is to achieve a nice golden brown color, not to scorch the meat.

5. When the roast has been browned, remove it from the pot and let it rest on a plate. Add all the vegetables from the marinade to the drippings, and cook on medium heat for 5 minutes, stirring occasionally.

6. Push the vegetables up against the sides of the casserole, and place the roast in the empty area in the center. The goal is to have the roast surrounded by vegetables on all sides. Add enough broth to come halfway up the sides of the roast. Add the crushed salt.

7. Bring the casserole to a simmer over medium heat. While the pot is coming to a simmer, preheat the oven to 250 degrees. When the pot has reached a steady simmer, cover, and place it in the preheated oven. Let it cook for 1 hour.

8. Remove the casserole from the oven, and turn the roast over. Cover, and return the roast to the oven. Cook for 1 more hour. Remove the roast from the oven, and test for doneness by sticking a big fork or skewer into the meat. If it goes in easily, the meat is done. If not, return to the oven, and check for doneness at 15 minute intervals.

9. Remove the roast from the pot, put on a plate, and let rest in a warm place. If the gravy is thin, reduce it by boiling for 10 minutes. You want it to be thick enough to coat a spoon. After the liquid is boiled down, reduce to a simmer, add the arrowroot mixture and mix well. At this point you can serve the gravy just as it is, or you can puree the vegetables into the sauce with a hand blender. It will be wonderful either way.

Slice the roast, and serve with the gravy. Enjoy these wonderful traditional flavors.

NOTE: If you want to cook the meat on the same day, marinate the meat for 2 hours at room temperature and proceed to Step 4.

Gypsy Pot Roast, Bohemian Style

The gypsies, also known as Romany, are a people of mysterious origin who have wandered Europe, especially central and southeastern Europe, for centuries. Some scholars believe they came from India. That theory finds some support in the spice mixture for this dish, which includes spices commonly used in Indian cuisine. The spice mixture is used in several traditional central European dishes which have the word "gypsy" somewhere in their title. This particular mixture is from Bohemia. Regardless of where the spice mixture is from, it really brings out the flavor of good beef, and provides a superbly flavorful gravy.

Serves 3 to 6

1 (2 to 4 pound) chuck roast, (or rump, or bottom round)

Spice Mixture

1 tablespoon organic (or the equivalent) sweet paprika, (I use Spanish paprika, grown in the traditional way)

½ teaspoon organic (or the equivalent) hot paprika

1 teaspoon freshly ground organic black pepper

½ teaspoon Jamaican allspice

¼ teaspoon organic ground cloves

For Pre-Browning

2 tablespoons pastured butter

1 teaspoon coarse unrefined sea salt, crushed

For Pot Roasting

2 large organic onions, chopped

2 large organic carrots, peeled and cut into 2 inch pieces

1 to 2 cups good homemade bone broth, such as *Quadruple Healing Broth* (page 52)

2 tablespoons pastured butter, thinly sliced

1 tablespoon arrowroot, mixed with 1 tablespoon filtered water

1. Mix the paprika, pepper, allspice, and cloves to make the spice mixture. Mix well.

2. Melt the butter in a cast iron casserole over medium heat. Rub the salt all over the roast. When the butter is hot and slightly smoking, brown the roast on all sides. You want it to be browned, not scorched.

3. When the roast is brown on all sides, place it in the center of the casserole. Surround the roast with the onions and the carrots. Add enough broth to come halfway up the side of the roast. Add the spice mixture to the broth. Mix well. Place the sliced butter on top of the roast. Bring the liquid to a simmer, and cover.

4. Simmer for 1 hour. The simmering could take anywhere from 1 to 2½ hours, depending on the size of the roast and how tender it is. Test for doneness by sticking a big fork or skewer into the meat. If it goes in easily, the meat is done.

5. When the roast is ready, remove it from the pot, and let it rest in a warm place.

6. Look at the liquid remaining in the pot. If it is thin, (most likely), turn up the heat to high, and boil it down for about 5 minutes. Don't worry if the onions and carrots disintegrate into the sauce. That is good, as it will make the gravy even more flavorful. Turn the heat down to medium. Add the arrowroot mixture, and stir into the sauce. If it isn't thick enough, sprinkle in some more arrowroot and stir. The gravy is thick enough when it coats the back of a spoon.

Serve, and enjoy the marvelous flavors.

Pot Roast with Wild Mushrooms, in the Style of Poland

Polish cooking deserves to be better known, because it is superb. The Poles have traditionally loved meat, and would often combine their grassfed beef with the magnificent wild mushrooms of Poland, one of the treasures of Polish cuisine. This recipe is better if you use Polish Borowiki mushrooms (they are available through the Internet), but it will be sensational with any good European wild mushrooms, such as porcini, or mixed wild mushrooms. The gravy is so wonderful that you will be tempted to lick your plate.

Serves 3 to 6

1 (3 pound) rump roast

For the Mushrooms
1 ounce dried wild mushrooms, (preferably Borowiki or porcini), sliced
1 cup hot filtered water

For Pre-Browning
2 tablespoons pastured butter

For Pot Roasting
2 tablespoons pastured butter
2 large organic onions, sliced
2 teaspoons coarse unrefined sea salt, crushed
1 teaspoon freshly ground organic black pepper
1 teaspoon organic dried marjoram, crushed between your fingers
1 cup good homemade broth, such as *Beef Broth* (page 45)
1 tablespoon arrowroot, mixed with 1 tablespoon filtered water

1. Two hours before you plan to cook the pot roast, place the dried mushrooms in a glass bowl, and cover with hot filtered water.

2. In a cast iron casserole, melt the butter over medium heat, until hot and slightly smoking. Brown the meat on all sides, turning often, so no scorching occurs. Put the meat on a plate to rest while you prepare the rest of the ingredients. (You could even brown the meat the day before you cook the roast, and refrigerate it overnight. If you do, let the meat cool before you cover and refrigerate it. Be sure to let it come to room temperature before you cook it.)

3. Melt the remaining 2 tablespoons of butter over medium heat. When the butter is hot and slightly smoking, add the onions, and cook for about 15 minutes, until they are soft and caramelized.

4. When the mushrooms have soaked for 2 hours, remove the mushrooms from their liquid, and add to the onions, mixing well. Strain the remaining liquid, and reserve. Turn the heat down to low, and cook for 5 minutes.

5. Preheat the oven to 300 degrees. Rub the salt, pepper, and marjoram into the roast. Place the roast in the casserole, and surround with the onions and mushrooms. Add ½ cup of the strained liquid into the pot. Add the broth. Bring the mixture to a simmer over the stove, cover, and place in the preheated oven. Cook for 30 minutes.

6. Turn the heat down to 250 degrees, and cook for 1 more hour. Test for doneness by sticking a big fork or skewer into the meat. If it goes in easily, the meat is done. If the meat is not tender enough, continue cooking at 250 degrees, testing for doneness at 15 minute intervals.

7. When the meat is done, remove the roast from the casserole, heat the gravy to a simmer, and thicken with the arrowroot mixture.

Serve, and enjoy the wonderful flavors.

Central European Pot Roast with Mushrooms

Pot roast is a favorite in dozens of European countries. While each country has several variations, the basic idea is the same. A big piece of chewy, but flavorful meat is browned in hot fat, then cooked gently with various vegetables, spices, and broth. If done right, the meat becomes beautifully tender, and picks up a lot of flavor from the other cooking ingredients. The vegetables, spices, and broth cook down to form a wonderful gravy. This recipe combines German and Polish flavors with American grassfed meat. As usual, grassfed meat cooks faster, shrinks less, and has more flavor of its own. It is absolutely delicious, and just good eating.

Serves 4 to 6

1 (3 pound) boneless chuck roast

For Pre-Browning
1 ounce dried wild mushrooms, such as porcini, or shiitake
Hot filtered water
2 tablespoons pastured butter

For Pot Roasting
1 medium organic onion, sliced
2 organic carrots, peeled and roughly chopped
1 organic leek, (or 4 organic green onions), cleaned and roughly chopped
3 stalks organic celery, roughly chopped
½ bunch organic Italian parsley, with stems, roughly chopped
1 to 2 cups good homemade broth, such as *Beef Broth* (page 45)
1 teaspoon coarse unrefined sea salt, crushed
½ teaspoon freshly ground organic black pepper
1 tablespoon arrowroot, mixed with 1 tablespoon filtered water

1. Take the meat out of the refrigerator about 1 hour before you plan to cook it, so it can reach room temperature.

2. Put the mushrooms in a bowl just large enough to hold them, and cover with hot filtered water. The mushrooms should soak for 1 hour so they can soften.

3. Melt the butter over medium heat in a cast iron casserole. When the butter is hot and slightly smoking, brown the roast on all sides over medium heat. This could take 8 to 14 minutes, depending on the size of the roast. When the roast is browned, remove it from the heat, and put it on a plate to rest. (If you prefer, you can do this step the night before, but it is not necessary. If you do, let the meat cool before you cover and refrigerate it. Be sure to let it come to room temperature before Step 5.)

4. While the roast is resting, clean and chop the vegetables.

5. Preheat the oven to 300 degrees. In the same casserole in which you browned the roast, heat the drippings over medium heat. When the drippings are hot, cook the onions for 5 minutes, or until they have softened.

6. Place the roast on the onions, and surround the roast with the other vegetables. Add enough broth to come halfway up the sides of the roast. Add the salt and pepper to the broth. Bring the pot to a simmer, cover, and place in the oven. Cook for 45 minutes.

7. Turn the roast over, cover, and return to the oven. Cook for another 45 minutes. Test for doneness by sticking a big fork or skewer into the meat. If it goes in easily, the meat is done. If the meat is not done, test for doneness at 10 minute intervals.

8. When the roast is done, remove the pot from the oven, and put it on the stove. Remove the meat from the pot, and put it in a warm place. Bring the remaining contents of the pot to a simmer, and thicken with the arrowroot mixture to the consistency you prefer.

You will have a delicious gravy to serve with your pot roast.

Nutritious Stew,
Inspired by Dr. Weston A. Price

Dr. Weston A. Price[1] was one of the most important people who ever walked this earth. Dr. Price was a dentist who noticed that each generation of his patients was less healthy than the preceding one. He suspected that poor nutrition was the cause. Dr. Price traveled around the world to study the eating patterns of traditional populations. He found that those groups who ate their traditional, natural diets were healthy, and almost completely free of disease. But when some of these people changed to a Western diet of processed, refined foods, they became unhealthy. They suffered many chronic diseases, such as heart disease and cancer which had been extremely rare with a traditional diet.

Dr. Price shared his knowledge by writing *Nutrition and Physical Degeneration*, a book that described his travels, his research, and provided invaluable information on healthy eating. Dr. Price described an experiment which proved to be of great benefit to a group of 27 children at a mission school. These children were selected because they had horrible teeth, full of cavities. During the experiment, Dr. Price gave those children one excellent meal per day, based on his principles of nutrition. The children's health benefitted greatly from this meal. Their teeth improved. Even their schoolwork improved.

The main part of the meal was a very nutritious meat dish, containing bone marrow and many vegetables, including carrots. The description of this dish and its preparation is incomplete, but enough information was provided for me to attempt to create something similar. My version is absolutely delicious, and extremely nutritious. Eating this will leave you refreshed and energized.

Dr. Price cooked the meat separately from the rest of the ingredients before combining them, so the meat would not be overcooked. His method of cooking the meat is described as "broiled." I have found that pan broiling works best, and does not overcook the meat. Don't be intimidated by the length of the recipe. It's actually simple to prepare, once you're familiar with the recipe.

Serves 4 to 6

---

1   The best sources of information on Dr. Price and his work are the Weston A. Price Foundation (www.westonaprice.org) and the Price-Pottenger Nutrition Foundation (www.ppnf.org).

For the Beef

> 1 (3 pound) center cut shoulder roast, or cross rib, sirloin tip, or any tender cut of meat. (Alternatively, you can use steaks from these cuts.)
>
> 3 tablespoons pastured butter

For the Base

> 1 pound beef marrow bones, cut so you can scoop out the marrow
>
> 1 cup cool filtered water
>
> ¼ cup pastured butter
>
> 1 pound organic carrots, peeled and coarsely chopped
>
> 1 pound organic onions, peeled and coarsely chopped
>
> 3 stalks organic celery, coarsely chopped
>
> 1 bunch organic Italian parsley, finely chopped
>
> 1 pound organic potatoes, peeled and diced, (approximately ½ inch cubes)
>
> 1 teaspoon coarse unrefined sea salt
>
> 3 cups homemade *Beef Broth* (page 45)

Cooking the Beef

1. If using a roast, cut it into 1 inch slices. Dry each slice thoroughly.

2. Melt 3 tablespoons butter in a large cast iron frying pan over medium heat. When the mixture is bubbly and slightly smoking, sauté the beef slices 3 minutes on each side. Do this in batches, so you do not crowd the slices together while they are sautéing.

3. Set the beef slices aside to rest.

Cooking the Base

4. Soak the marrow bones in 1 cup cool, filtered water.

5. Melt the butter over medium heat in a large cast iron frying pan. When the butter is bubbly and slightly smoking, add the carrots, onions, celery, and parsley to the pan, and sauté gently for 10 minutes, stirring occasionally to make sure the vegetables are well mixed.

6. Add the potatoes and mix well. Remove from the heat.

7. Remove the marrow bones from the water. Carefully remove the marrow from the bone, carefully running over the marrow with your fingers to remove any bone fragments. Finely chop the marrow. (Reserve the bones for a future broth.) Add the marrow, salt, and beef broth to the pan with the vegetables. Bring to a simmer, and mix well. Cover, and simmer for 1 hour.

Final Touches

8. After the base has simmered for 1 hour, finely chop all the beef slices, being sure to save all the juice that runs out.

9. Add the chopped meat and its juices to the stew base. Simmer until heated through, which should only take a couple of minutes.

Enjoy, and be healthy!

Beef Stew with Bone Marrow

What did the cavemen prefer to eat above all else? They left a record that answered the question. Just about every site where early humans lived features a large pile of animal bones, which must have come from the hunt. Just about every leg bone in these piles has been cracked open, apparently with rocks. Cracking these bones open must have been hard work. Why did they do it? They must have wanted the bone marrow. Why did they want the bone marrow so much?

Bone marrow is a nutritional treasure, just bursting with health-giving substances. It also gives a wonderful flavor to food. When combined with bone broth, organic vegetables, and grassfed meat, it creates a gravy that tastes so good, you can't stop eating it. This stew is quite simple, and so delicious. Be sure that you have some bread available to mop up the gravy, or you may feel compelled to lick your plate. It's that good.

Serves 2 to 4

> 1 to 1½ pounds stew beef, either in one piece or cubed
>
> 1 pound beef marrow bones, cut so you can scoop out the marrow
>
> Cool filtered water
>
> 2 tablespoons pastured butter
>
> 3 organic carrots, peeled and coarsely chopped
>
> 3 stalks organic celery, coarsely chopped
>
> 1 medium organic onion, coarsely chopped
>
> 3 medium organic potatoes, peeled and cut into 1½ inch cubes
>
> 2 cups good homemade broth, such as *Beef* or *Nomad's Broth* (pages 45 - 53)
>
> 1 teaspoon coarse unrefined sea salt, crushed
>
> ½ teaspoon organic freshly ground black pepper
>
> 1 tablespoon arrowroot, mixed with 1 tablespoon filtered water

1. Put the marrow bones in a bowl of cool, filtered water that is large and deep enough to just cover them.
2. Heat the butter over medium heat in a heavy pan. When the butter is hot and slightly smoking, brown the meat on all sides.
3. Let the meat rest and the bones soak for 1 hour. You can peel and chop the vegetables during this period.
4. Remove the marrow bones from the water. Carefully remove the marrow from the bone, carefully running over the marrow with your fingers to remove any bone fragments. Break the bone marrow into little crumbly pieces. (Reserve the bones for a future broth.)
5. If the meat was in one piece, chop it into cubes. Place the meat, bone marrow, vegetables, broth, salt and pepper in a cast iron casserole and mix well. Preheat the oven to 250 degrees.
6. Bring the mixture to a strong simmer, cover the casserole, and place it in the oven. Cook for 1 to 1½ hours, or until tender. Thicken the gravy with the arrowroot mixture.

Serve, and enjoy the wonderful flavors.

Grassfed Steak Kew

Steak Kew was a popular dish in American Chinese restaurants during the '50s and '60s. It probably was created for American tastes and ingredients. Whatever its origin, Steak Kew is wonderful. The combination of sautéed tenderloin cubes, mushrooms, oyster sauce, ginger, garlic, and other flavors is just delicious. I first tasted Steak Kew in 1965, in a long vanished Chinese restaurant in Concord, California. It immediately became one of my favorites, and I had it many times until the restaurant closed. I then tried to recreate it, and after much experimentation, succeeded. Of course, that was with factory beef. My switch to grassfed beef required me to redo the recipe. I also wanted to see if it could be made without soy. This recipe breaks the usual rule of not cooking beef at more than medium heat. It succeeds because the ginger really tenderizes the meat. Made with quality organic ingredients, this version is the best ever.

Serves 2 to 4

1 pound tenderloin kebabs or tips, cut into ½ to 1 inch cubes or rectangles

For the Marinade

2 tablespoons Thai fish sauce, (I use Thai Kitchen brand)

2 tablespoons natural (no MSG) oyster sauce

1 teaspoon freshly ground organic black pepper

¼ teaspoon organic hot sauce

1 (1 inch) cube organic fresh ginger, finely chopped

2 large organic garlic cloves, finely chopped

2 large green onions, finely chopped

For Stir-Frying

2 tablespoons organic extra virgin olive oil, (or non-hydrogenated lard)

¼ pound organic snow peas, strings removed, (or 1 bunch green onions, chopped into 1 inch lengths)

½ pound fresh shiitake mushrooms, (or crimini), sliced

1. Combine the marinade ingredients in a glass bowl. Mix well. Add the meat, and mix well. Marinate at least 2 hours at room temperature, or cover and refrigerate overnight.

2. If you refrigerated the meat, remove it from the refrigerator at least 1 hour before you plan to cook it, so it can come to room temperature.

3. Heat the cooking fat over medium high heat until it is hot and slightly smoking. Stir-fry the meat cubes for 1 minute, or until all the red color is gone. Remove the meat from the pan.

4. Add the vegetables to the pan, and stir-fry for 2 minutes. Return the meat to the pan, and stir-fry everything together for 1 more minute.

Serve and enjoy.

Stir-Fried Beef with Mushrooms and Onions, Vietnamese Style

Beef has an honored place in Vietnamese cooking. Some Vietnamese restaurants serve a meal that consists of no less than seven different beef courses — now that's appreciation. I put this recipe together using my favorite Vietnamese ingredients, and adding mushrooms. The results were terrific. You can use a variety of cuts for this dish, from the moderately tender, such as shoulder, to tenderloin, the ultimate in tenderness. Whatever you use, the marinade will tenderize it, and infuse it with great flavor. The Thai fish sauce really brings out and deepens the flavor of the meat, without a fishy taste. Olive oil works beautifully in this stir-fry. Once again, we cook the beef at medium high heat, instead of medium. The large amount of black pepper gives it a very flavorful heat that is different from the usual hot red peppers. This one is fairly spicy, great for hot weather.

Serves 2 to 4

1 pound center cut shoulder, (or sirloin tip)

For the Marinade
2 organic green onions, white part only, finely chopped
1 (1 inch) piece of fresh organic ginger, finely chopped
4 large cloves of organic garlic, finely chopped
2 teaspoons freshly ground organic black pepper
2 tablespoons Thai fish sauce, (I use Thai Kitchen brand)
1 tablespoon organic unrefined brown sugar, such as Rapadura
1 tablespoon toasted sesame oil
¼ teaspoon thick red organic hot sauce
1 teaspoon organic cornstarch

For Stir-Frying Meat
2 tablespoons organic extra virgin olive oil

For Stir-Frying Vegetables
1 tablespoon organic extra virgin olive oil
1 large organic onion, sliced
8 ounces fresh sliced mushrooms, either crimini or shiitake

1. At least 1 hour before you plan to cook the beef, trim off any connective tissue, and cut the meat into small rectangles about ½ inch thick. Mix the marinade ingredients well. Combine them in a glass bowl with the beef, making sure that the beef is well coated with the marinade. Let marinate at room temperature for 1 hour.

2. Heat 2 tablespoons of the olive oil over medium high heat in a large cast iron frying pan. When the oil is hot and bubbly, stir-fry the marinated beef for about 1 minute, or until all pieces have lost their red color. Remove the beef to a bowl.

3. Add the remaining tablespoon of olive oil to the hot pan. Add the onions and mushrooms, and stir-fry over medium high heat until the mushrooms have browned, and the onions have softened. This should take 2 to 4 minutes.

4. Add the beef to the vegetable mixture, mix well, and serve.

Pan Kebabs

Shish kebab is a very old dish that takes many forms. It usually consists of cubed meat, marinated and placed on skewers with various vegetables, then cooked over a fire. Shish kebab is popular in many Mediterranean countries. In Russia, it is known as shashlik, and originated in the Caucasus region. Since I've always had trouble with skewers, I decided to see if this dish could be made on a frying pan, without the hassle. It certainly can. I used traditional Caucasian flavors in the marinade, and traditional shish kebab vegetables. The results? Mmmmmm. You have to try this one.

Serves 2 to 4

1 pound beef tenderloin, (or ribeye, sirloin, or center cut shoulder), cut for kebabs (½ to 1 inch cubes)

For the Marinade
1 small onion, grated or pureed, with the liquid

2 tablespoons natural pomegranate concentrate

¼ cup unfiltered organic extra virgin olive oil

2 tablespoons filtered water

1 teaspoon freshly ground organic black pepper

1 teaspoon organic dried basil

4 cloves organic garlic, finely chopped

For Stir-Frying the Meat
2 tablespoons organic extra virgin olive oil

For Stir-Frying the Vegetables
1 tablespoon organic extra virgin olive oil

1 organic onion, cut into wedges, then separated into individual leaves

1 organic green pepper, cut into 1 inch squares

1 organic tomato, thinly sliced, (allow the juice to drain away)

1. The night before you plan to cook the kebabs, mix the marinade ingredients well. Put the meat in a glass bowl, add the marinade, and stir, making sure all the meat is well coated. Cover and let rest at room temperature for 1 hour, then refrigerate overnight.

2. An hour before you plan to cook the kebabs, take them out of the refrigerator so they can come to room temperature.

3. Heat 2 tablespoons olive oil in a cast iron frying pan over medium heat. Remove the kebabs from the marinade, and let drain.

4. When the oil is hot, bubbly, and slightly smoking, add the meat, and stir until all surfaces have been lightly browned, about 1 to 2 minutes. Remove the beef from the pan.

5. Turn up the heat to medium high, adding 1 more tablespoon of olive oil. Add the vegetables, and stir for 1 to 2 minutes, until the onions and the peppers are lightly browned. Turn off the heat, return the meat to the pan, mix well, and serve.

This tastes so good that you won't miss the skewers.

Goulash Stir-Fry

Most people associate stir-frying with Chinese cooking. However, the technique can work very well with European style ingredients. This dish uses traditional Hungarian flavors to create an absolutely delicious, and extremely nourishing breakfast dish.

Here are two variations. The bacon variation is more Hungarian in flavor, but the butter version is also superb. This is a quick dish.

Serves 2

½ **pound top sirloin, or center cut shoulder**

For the Marinade
1 **tablespoon unfiltered organic extra virgin olive oil**

For Stir-Frying
1 **medium organic onion**
¼ **pound crimini mushrooms**
2 **organic eggs**
2 **tablespoons pastured butter, (see bacon variation below)**
1 **teaspoon Hungarian sweet paprika**
¼ **teaspoon coarse unrefined sea salt, crushed**
¼ **teaspoon freshly ground black pepper**

1. Slice the beef against the grain into ¼ inch slices. Cut the slices into thin strips, no more than 2 inches long. Mix the meat with the olive oil in a glass bowl, cover, and refrigerate overnight.

2. An hour before you plan to cook the meat, remove it from the refrigerator so that it can come to room temperature.

3. Thinly slice the onion and the mushrooms. Break the eggs into a bowl, and mix well with a fork.

4. Melt the butter in a cast iron frying pan over medium heat. When the butter is hot and slightly smoking, cook the onions and mushrooms together until the onions have softened, and the mushrooms have browned, which should take about 5 minutes. Add the beef slices. Sprinkle the spices on the mixture. Stir until the beef has lost its red color.

5. Pour in the eggs, stirring constantly. Serve as soon as the eggs are cooked.

Bacon Variation
Omit the butter. Add 2 slices of good natural bacon to a cold cast iron frying pan. Turn the heat to medium and cook, turning occasionally, until the bacon has rendered most of its fat to the pan. Remove the bacon from the pan. Cook as above, using the bacon fat in the pan, instead of the butter. When the dish is cooked, crumble the bacon and stir it into the mixture.

Portuguese Beef in the Style of Migas

Portuguese cuisine is not that well known, which is a shame, because there are some great traditional dishes. Migas is usually made with a combination of beef and pork, with bacon and a sautéed bread stuffing. Here we just use beef. Portuguese beef, like most European beef, is traditionally grassfed, so American grassfed tenderloin works just fine. The flavors are unusual and superb.

Serves 2 to 4

1 pound tenderloin kebabs or tips, cut into ½ to 1 inch cubes or rectangles

For the Marinade

1½ tablespoons sweet (dulce) paprika, preferably Portuguese or Spanish
1 teaspoon organic garlic powder
1 teaspoon freshly ground organic black pepper
2 tablespoons unfiltered organic extra virgin olive oil

For Stir-Frying

½ teaspoon coarse unrefined sea salt, crushed
2 tablespoons organic olive oil

1. An hour before you plan to cook the migas, combine the paprika, garlic powder, black pepper, and unfiltered olive oil to make a marinade. Mix well with the beef. Let the marinated beef rest in a covered glass bowl for at least 1 hour at room temperature, or refrigerate overnight.

2. If you refrigerated the beef, remove it from the refrigerator at least 1 hour before you plan to cook it, so it can come to room temperature.

3. Right before you start cooking, mix the salt with the marinated beef.

4. Heat the oil in a cast iron skillet over medium heat until it is hot, bubbly, and slightly smoking. Carefully dump the migas into the hot oil, and fry, stirring occasionally, until all sides are lightly browned. This should take 1 to 2 minutes, and should give you meat that is pink to medium rare, depending on the size of the pieces.

Serve, and enjoy the delicious flavors.

Beef Stroganoff

Meat with mushrooms, onions, and sour cream has long been a tradition in Eastern Europe. The combination of flavors can be sublime. The most famous dish of this type is Beef Stroganoff. This dish was created for a certain Prince Stroganoff, the head of one of Russia's most powerful and wealthy families, who was said to own 40,000 serfs. I hesitate to call the dish Russian, because the writers of some traditional Russian cookbooks have pointed out how "unrussian" the dish actually is. Curiously enough, Beef Stroganoff is the most famous of all Russian recipes. But after researching a number of sources, I believe it is most likely Hungarian.

Whatever its origin, whenever I tried to make this dish for my wife in years past, I found it lacking. I have since learned what was missing — grassfed beef, rich homemade broth, and organic sour cream. All of the missing ingredients are in this recipe, and we love it.

The original recipe calls for tenderloin. I think tenderloin was put in there just to be extravagant, so Prince Stroganoff could show off. Other cuts are far better in this recipe. I doubt that Prince Stroganoff used shiitake mushrooms, but they are wonderful in this dish. He didn't use garlic or parsley either, but the dish is much better with them.

Serves 2 to 4

1 pound sirloin tip, (or sirloin, or tri-tip)

10 dried shiitake mushrooms, (you can substitute ½ pound fresh shiitake or crimini mushrooms, sliced)

Hot filtered water

3 tablespoons pastured butter

1 medium organic onion, roughly chopped

4 large cloves organic garlic, peeled and chopped

8 sprigs organic Italian parsley, finely chopped

1 cup homemade *Beef Broth* (page 45)

½ teaspoon coarse unrefined sea salt, crushed

1 teaspoon freshly ground organic black pepper

1 teaspoon arrowroot

½ cup organic sour cream

1. Place the dried shiitake mushrooms in a bowl. Cover with hot filtered water. Soak for 20 minutes. (Omit this step if using fresh mushrooms.)

2. Cut the beef into thin strips, about 2 inches long, ¼ inch wide, ¼ inch thick.

3. Drain the mushrooms, and cut into thin strips, discarding the tough knob in the center.

4. Melt the butter in a cast iron frying pan over medium heat. When the butter is hot and slightly smoking, lightly brown the meat in batches to avoid overcrowding. Remove each batch to a plate once it has been lightly browned.

5. When all the meat has been browned, add the mushrooms, onion, garlic, and parsley to the pan. Sauté over medium heat for 5 minutes.

6. Return the browned meat to the pan. Add the broth, salt, and pepper. Mix well. Bring to a simmer, cover, and simmer for 15 minutes.

7. Mix the arrowroot into the sour cream. When the 15 minutes are up, add the sour cream/arrowroot mixture to the pan. Mix well, and bring to a slow simmer, uncovered.

Serve immediately. Enjoy.

Grassfed Cheeseburger

Ground beef is the one area where there is not that much difference between cooking grassfed beef and other kinds of beef. It is also the area where the difference in taste, quality, and healthfulness may be the greatest. Since I don't want to spoil your appetite, I will simply say that factory ground beef is almost always made from the cheapest factory beef available. I used to dislike ground beef in all its forms, when I was eating factory beef. I now love hamburgers, cheeseburgers, meatloaf, and all kinds of ground meat dishes. The difference? Grassfed beef tastes so much better, has a better mouthfeel, and I feel good after eating it. Grassfed ground beef will cook a little bit faster, and it has a much better flavor which you may not want to mask with too many other ingredients. Just about any recipe for ground beef will work with grassfed beef. I decided not to include a lot of recipes for ground beef, because they are not needed.

Here is my recipe for an American institution — the cheeseburger. I use fewer ingredients because I want the great natural flavor of the meat to come through, complemented perfectly by the cheese.

Serves 4

1 pound grassfed ground beef, divided into 4 equal parts, and formed into patties about ½ inch thick

4 thin slices natural cheddar cheese, (preferably raw milk cheese), about the width of the patties

½ teaspoon fine RealSalt, (or 1 teaspoon coarse natural sea salt, crushed)

½ teaspoon organic freshly ground black pepper

½ teaspoon organic garlic powder

8 slices organic sourdough bread, about the width of the patties, (or 4 organic hamburger buns)

1 tablespoon pastured butter

1. Mix the seasonings, and sprinkle them over the meat.

2. Heat the butter over medium heat in a large frying pan until it is hot and slightly smoking. Cook the patties for 3 to 5 minutes on each side, depending on how you like them. Place a cheese slice on each patty for the last minute of cooking.

3. When the cheese has melted, place each patty on one of the sourdough slices, and top with the other sourdough slice.

Serve and enjoy.

Mushroom and Cream Meatloaf

As mentioned elsewhere, this book does not contain a lot of ground beef recipes, because most conventional recipes will work with grassfed ground beef. However, this recipe is so good that my wife (and editor), Keren, insisted that I put it in this book.

Long before I learned about grassfed beef, I used to enjoy a meatloaf made with canned cream of mushroom soup. I gave up using canned factory soup years ago, but got a craving for the meatloaf every now and then. The canned soup contained some form of cream, some form of mushrooms, and a vast array of chemicals, preservatives, and other artificial ingredients. The idea came to me — what if I used real mushrooms, real cream, real butter, grassfed beef, a few other natural ingredients, and left out the factory gunk? The result was this recipe. Try it and taste why I had to put it in this book.

Serves 4

For the Mushroom Base

3 tablespoons pastured butter

¼ pound fresh crimini or shiitake mushrooms, finely chopped

1 medium onion, peeled and finely chopped

½ cup fresh organic cream, (or raw cream)

1 teaspoon coarse unrefined sea salt, crushed

½ teaspoon freshly ground organic black pepper

For the Meatloaf

2 slices good natural bread, either sourdough or sprouted

1 pound grassfed ground beef

1 free range organic egg, slightly beaten

Grated organic cheese of your choice, enough to cover the top of the meatloaf

1. Melt the butter over medium high heat in a cast iron frying pan. When the butter is hot and slightly smoking, add the mushrooms and onions, and cook, stirring occasionally, until the mushrooms have browned and shrunk, which should take 2 to 4 minutes. Place the mixture in a bowl, and add the cream, salt, and pepper. Mix well.

2. Turn the bread into breadcrumbs, using a blender. Mix the crumbs with the meat and egg. Add the mushroom mixture to the meat, mixing well.

3. Preheat the oven to 400 degrees. Grease a glass quart sized loaf pan, using some good butter. Add the meatloaf mixture to the pan, and form into a loaf conforming to the shape of the pan. Cover the top of the loaf with the grated cheese. Place the pan in the preheated oven, and bake for 35 to 45 minutes, or until the top of the meatloaf is firm.

Serve and enjoy.

Tender
Grassfed Bison

About Grassfed Bison

Once, the Great Plains of the United States were home to huge herds of bison, numbering in the millions. In the nineteenth century, the bison were almost exterminated for their hides. The bison have made a huge comeback, and many are being raised for food.

Unfortunately, most of the bison meat sold in this country tastes like beef. This is a shame, because bison raised and finished on native grasses has a deep, wonderful flavor of its own, which is mild and delicious. However, the overwhelming majority of bison producers feed grain, soybeans, and "protein supplements" to their bison, which makes them grow faster and taste like conventional beef. Fortunately, there are a few ranchers who raise bison completely on grass, and finish them on grass.

All the bison I have seen in supermarkets has been finished on grain and supplements. You have to be very careful when shopping for bison, as producers of grain finished bison usually do not specify what they feed their herd. Fortunately, those ranchers who finish their bison on grass do make it clear that they only use grass. (See *Sources*, page 217.)

This book only covers the cooking of grassfed and grass finished bison. The best time to buy bison meat is in the spring through the fall, when the grass is green. The quality of the grass has a great effect on the taste of the meat.

Grassfed bison is one of the most satisfying meats you will ever eat. Grassfed bison is even leaner than grassfed beef. It can be very tender when cooked properly. Because the flavor of grassfed bison is so superb, my recipes are designed to bring out that flavor, rather than hide it.

Cooking Tender Bison

Some people believe that you can cook grassfed bison just like grassfed beef. This has not been my experience. If you cook bison as if it were beef, you will most likely be disappointed. That would be a shame, because bison is wonderful when cooked right. Properly cooked bison is also very tender.

Grassfed Bison Is Different than Grassfed Beef

- It is leaner.
- It has little or no marbling.
- It has a deep, wonderful taste of its own.
- It has a somewhat different, softer texture.
- It does not respond well to salting before cooking, even if it is salted just before cooking.
- It needs very little in terms of seasoning to taste wonderful. Most seasonings just mask its great natural taste.

Bison Cooking Techniques

Because bison is different, it requires somewhat different cooking techniques. The main points to keep in mind are these:

1. **Bison steaks and roasts should always be marinated before cooking.**

   I get the best results from unfiltered, organic, extra virgin olive oil. The enzymes in the unfiltered oil bring out the flavor of the meat, while tenderizing it and improving the texture. Bison should be marinated overnight, or for several hours at room temperature. It needs longer marinating times than beef. If you marinate it for two days in the refrigerator, it will be even more tender.

2. **Bison steaks should never be salted before cooking.**

   While I will salt grassfed beef just before cooking, I have learned not to do this with bison. Pre-salting really toughens the meat. The early explorers remarked on the fact that the Native Americans never salted bison before cooking. Some of them also wrote that the meat did not need the salt. I agree.

3. **Grassfed bison cooks even more quickly than grassfed beef.**

4. **Bison steaks should never be cooked at high heat.**

   These steaks should not be cooked beyond medium. They should be watched carefully, and removed from the heat when done.

5. **The High-Low Method works well with bison roasts.**

   Bison roasts can be cooked briefly at high heat, just long enough to seal the roast. They must be finished on a much lower heat. These roasts can cook very quickly.

6. **Bison steaks and roasts are at their best when they are rare or medium rare.**

   Properly marinated and cooked bison steak or roast will be tender even when pink.

7. **The great taste of bison should not be hidden by too much seasoning**.

   Bison pot roasts and stews can be seasoned with various vegetables such as onions, leeks, green onions, garlic, parsley, carrots, and fruits such as blueberries or figs. Most other herbs and spices will overwhelm the great natural flavor of the meat, and should be avoided.

8. **Bison pot roasts and stews will also cook much more quickly than beef.**

9. **Bison roasts and pot roasts should always be sliced against the grain.**

   This will make the meat even more tender.

These principles are used in the following recipes, and they work. The recipes are simple. If you follow them, you will enjoy tender grassfed bison.

Judging Doneness in Grassfed Bison

Bison is ready at a lower temperature than beef. The cooking times given in this book are an estimate, based on experience. This is why variable times are given for so many recipes. These times should give excellent results for most grassfed bison. Do not be afraid to change the cooking times, based on your experience. You must get a feel for your cooking equipment, your oven, and the particular kind of bison you are cooking.

Judging Doneness

If you are cooking a roast, a good quality instant read meat thermometer can really help you judge the doneness of the meat, and how fast it is cooking. The ease with which the thermometer goes into the meat can also give you a good idea of how tender the meat is.

> **Doneness for Grassfed Bison:**
> Rare   110 - 120 degrees
> Medium Rare   121 - 125 degrees
> Medium   126 - 130 degrees
> Bison is at its best when rare, or medium rare.

A meat thermometer does not work for steaks, because the meat is not thick enough.

Another way of judging temperature is to stick a metal skewer or roasting fork into the meat, withdraw it, and test the temperature of the metal with your finger. If it is cool, the meat is not ready. If it is somewhat warm, it is rare. If it is slightly hot, it is medium rare. If it is hot, it is medium. Once you have enough experience at comparing the temperature of the metal with the doneness of the meat, you will know how done the meat is, according to your standards.

The ease with which the skewer or fork goes into the meat will give you a good idea of its tenderness.

Many cooking authorities will tell you to never pierce the meat while cooking, or you will "lose valuable juices." I have never found this to be true. Yes, sometimes some juice comes out, but it does not hurt the taste or juiciness of the meat.

Bison pot roasts are done when easily pierced with a skewer or fork. The easier it goes in, the more tender the meat.

Pan Broiled Bison Ribeye Steak

Grassfed bison is a very lean meat. It can be tough, if not properly cooked. Here we cook bison steak in a way that not only brings out its terrific flavor, but makes it very tender. Bison is at its best when it is rare, but this steak will be tender even if you cook it to the pink stage. This steak is particularly tender due to the use of tenderizing vegetables. The marinade is absolutely crucial to this recipe. So is the sautéing in butter. The combination of the two techniques yields a steak so tender and delicious that it needs nothing else.

Serves 3 to 4

2 pounds bison ribeye steaks, cut 1 to 1½ inch thick

For the Marinade

2 organic green onions, chopped and crushed
2 cloves organic garlic, chopped and crushed
1 (1 inch) piece of fresh organic ginger, chopped and crushed
3 tablespoons unfiltered organic extra virgin olive oil

For Sautéing

2 tablespoons pastured butter

1. At least 2 hours before you plan to cook the steaks, make the marinade by combining the green onions, garlic, and ginger with the olive oil. Coat the steaks on all sides with the marinade, pressing the vegetables into the meat. Let the steaks sit in the marinade at room temperature for at least 2 hours. (The steaks will be even more tender and flavorful if you let them rest for 1 hour at room temperature, then cover and refrigerate them overnight.)

2. If the steaks were refrigerated, take them out of the refrigerator about 1 hour before cooking, so they can come to room temperature.

3. Melt the butter in a cast iron frying pan over medium heat until hot and slightly smoking. Cook the bison steaks for 3 to 4 minutes on each side for rare, 4 to 5 minutes on each side for medium rare, depending on thickness.

4. When the steaks are done, remove them from the heat, and let them rest on a plate for 5 minutes.

Serve and enjoy.

Bone In Bison Rib Steak

Grassfed bison has a wonderful flavor all its own. That sweet, clean flavor is enhanced enormously when the steak is cooked with the bone. There is an old saying that the closer the meat is to the bone, the tastier it is. This is especially true for bison. Once again, no salt for bison. Here, the bone is the main spice for the meat. The bone releases marrow and other substances during cooking, which go right into the meat to give it an even deeper, more wonderful flavor.

Bison must be cooked carefully to be tender. This recipe will give you some very tender bison, flavored superbly by its own bone. This dish, despite its simplicity, is luxury fare.

Serves 2

1 bone in bison rib steak, about 1½ inches thick

For the Marinade
3 tablespoons unfiltered organic extra virgin olive oil

For Sautéing
2 tablespoons pastured butter

1. The night before you plan to cook the steak, pour the olive oil over all surfaces, and rub it in. Let rest in a glass bowl for 1 hour at room temperature, then cover and refrigerate overnight.

2. Take the steak out of the refrigerator at least 1 hour before you plan to cook it, so it can come to room temperature.

3. Heat the butter over medium heat in a large cast iron frying pan. When the oil is hot and slightly smoking, place the steak in the pan. Cook for 5 minutes on each side for rare, 6 to 7 minutes on each side for medium rare.

Serve and enjoy the deep, rich flavor of bone in bison.

Bison Tenderloin Steak

This is the most tender cut of the bison. It is also one of the leanest parts of the already lean bison. Because it is so lean, it needs a little help to bring out its great flavor, and to reach its peak of tenderness. This simple marinade accomplishes the task. The traditional European way to cook a tenderloin steak was to sauté it in butter, and that tradition works very well with bison tenderloin. Serving a tenderloin steak with a fried egg on top is a tradition all over northern and eastern Europe. The yolk of the egg provides a perfect natural sauce for the tender bison, and the combination is so good that you will understand why it has stood the test of time. This is a very special meal for two.

Serves 2

2 (8 ounce) bison tenderloin steaks, 1½ to 2 inches thick

For the Marinade
2 tablespoons unfiltered organic extra virgin olive oil
½ teaspoon organic onion powder
½ teaspoon freshly ground organic black pepper

For Sautéing
2 tablespoons pastured butter
2 large organic eggs

1. The day before you plan to cook the steaks, combine the oil, onion powder, and pepper, and rub all over the steaks. Let sit at room temperature for 1 hour, then cover and refrigerate overnight.

2. Take the steaks out of the refrigerator 1 hour before you plan to cook them, so they can come to room temperature.

3. Heat the butter over medium heat in a cast iron frying pan. When the butter is hot and slightly smoking, sauté the steaks for 2 to 4 minutes on each side, depending on their thickness and how you like them. While the steaks are cooking, fry the eggs in butter. Be sure to leave the yolks somewhat runny, so they can form a sauce for the steak. When the steaks and eggs are ready, top each steak with an egg, and serve.

Enjoy the great flavors of old Europe.

Pan Broiled Bison Strip Steak

Bison has a great flavor of its own, if grassfed. Bison is even leaner than grassfed beef. This means that it must be cooked very carefully to make it tender. I almost never use salt on bison, at any stage of the cooking, as it tends to toughen the meat. Traditionally, Native Americans did not use salt when cooking bison. Fortunately, the great flavor of bison needs no help.

I do not recommend cooking bison steak beyond medium rare. This recipe is actually very simple, but must be followed carefully to ensure that the meat is tender. A tender, juicy bison steak is one of the best meat experiences on the planet. This recipe brings out the sweet, natural goodness of the bison.

Serves 2 to 4

2 pounds bison strip steaks, about 1 to 1¼ inch thick

For the Marinade
2 tablespoons unfiltered organic extra virgin olive oil

For Sautéing
2 tablespoons pastured butter

1. The night before you plan to cook the steaks, combine them with the olive oil in a glass bowl. Rub the oil into the steaks, covering all surfaces. Let sit for 1 hour at room temperature, then cover and refrigerate overnight.

2. Take the meat out of the refrigerator at least 1 hour before you plan to cook it, so it can come to room temperature.

3. Heat the butter over medium heat in a large cast iron frying pan. When the butter is hot and slightly smoking, place the steaks in the pan. Do not crowd the steaks. You can cook in batches if necessary.

4. Cook for 3 minutes on each side for rare, or 4 minutes on each side for medium rare.

Serve, and enjoy the clean, sweet taste of real bison.

Bison Strip Steak with Blueberry Marinade

The challenge — find a good bison steak marinade. Bison has a clean, sweet, natural flavor that can easily be overwhelmed by spices and marinades. This made my search for a good bison steak marinade somewhat challenging. The answer came from the traditions of the people who ate more bison than anyone else — the Native Americans who lived on the Great Plains. My research found that blueberries were often used when stewing bison. I first tried this combination in *Bison Blueberry Stew* (page 158), which turned out tender and delicious. I did not find any use of blueberries in marinades. I decided to gamble since the combination worked so well in the stew. True, the Native Americans did not use olive oil, but I thought it would help carry the flavor of the blueberries into the meat. The gamble paid off, big time. Make this recipe, and you'll taste why. The blueberries in the marinade do change the color of the meat somewhat, but the taste is worth it.

Serves 4

4 bison strip steaks, about ½ pound each, about 1 inch thick

For the Marinade

½ cup wild organic blueberries, fresh or frozen (thawed if frozen)
2 tablespoons filtered water
2 tablespoons unfiltered organic extra virgin olive oil

For Sautéing

2 tablespoons pastured butter

1. The day before you plan to cook the steaks, make the marinade. Add the water to the blueberries in a bowl. Crush the blueberries into the water with a sturdy fork. When the blueberries are well crushed, combine with the olive oil. Place the steaks in a glass bowl, cover with the marinade, and let rest at room temperature for 1 hour. Cover and refrigerate overnight.

2. About 1 hour before you plan to cook the steaks, remove them from the refrigerator so they can come to room temperature. When the hour is almost up, remove the steaks from the marinade. Wipe off as much of the marinade as you can.

3. Heat the butter over medium heat in a heavy frying pan, preferably cast iron. When the butter is hot and slightly smoking, cook the steaks for 3 to 4 minutes on each side, until they are done to your liking.

The blueberries really enhance the flavor of the bison.

Sautéed Bison Flat Iron Steak

Flat iron is cut from the tender part of the chuck. It has a big wad of sinew in the center. However, the meat to either side is tender and delicious, with lots of flavor. Such a simple, easy recipe, and such a good one.

Serves 2

1 bison flat iron steak, about 1 inch thick

For the Marinade
2 tablespoons unfiltered organic extra virgin olive oil

For Sautéing
2 tablespoons pastured butter

1. The day before you plan to cook the steak, rub all sides with the olive oil, place in a glass or ceramic bowl, and marinate for 1 hour. Cover and refrigerate overnight.

2. An hour before you plan to cook the steak, remove it from the refrigerator so it can come to room temperature.

3. Melt the butter in a cast iron frying pan over medium heat, until it is hot and slightly smoking.

4. Sauté the steak for 3 to 4 minutes on each side, depending on whether you want it rare or medium rare.

5. Remove from the pan, and cut the meat away from the center wad of sinew.

Serve, and enjoy the wonderful flavor of this tender meat.

Roast Prime Rib of Bison

Prime rib, also known as standing rib roast, has long been considered the king of beef roasts. This is definitely the king of bison roasts, perhaps the king of all roasts. Except for the olive oil marinade, this roast uses no seasoning except the natural bones and fat cover of the bison. This recipe really brings out the deep, clean, sweet flavor of grassfed bison. The unfiltered extra virgin olive oil makes it very tender. It would be a crime to mask this wonderful flavor with spices. No salt is needed. This particular cut has a unique, wonderful flavor all its own, which is so good and so satisfying.

The secret is in the marinating and the timing. This roast, like all bison, cooks very quickly. This recipe is quite simple. Follow it carefully, and you will be rewarded with the wonderful flavor of the king of bison roasts, prime rib.

Serves 3 to 4

1 (2½ to 3½ pound) bison standing rib roast, bone in, 2 ribs, with fat cap (see note below)

For the Marinade
3 tablespoons unfiltered organic extra virgin olive oil

1. The day before you plan to cook the roast, rub the oil into all the surfaces of the meat. Let sit for 1 hour at room temperature, then cover and refrigerate overnight.

2. At least 1 hour before you plan to cook the roast, take it out of the refrigerator so it can come to room temperature.

3. Preheat the oven to 425 degrees. Place the roast in a roasting pan, fat side up. Roast for 15 minutes.

4. Baste the roast with the pan drippings. Turn the oven down to 250 degrees. Cook for 20 minutes. Check for doneness. If the roast is not done, check for doneness at 5 minute intervals. The roast could take up to another 20 minutes, depending on its size and shape. Do not cook beyond medium rare.

Serve, and enjoy this true king of roasts.

NOTE: Feel free to put some sliced butter on top of the roast if it lacks a good fat cap.

Super-Tender Double Bison Chop

This method resulted in the most tender bison I ever had. It was absolutely delicious. The natural subtle sweetness of grassfed bison is really brought out by this recipe. I did not try cutting it with a fork — I was too busy eating it — but I could have.

This recipe came about by accident. I had ordered a 2-rib standing bison rib roast. My plan was to cut it into two big rib steaks. However, the roast came with a solid ridge of bone that no knife was going to cut through. It also had the entire top covered with the chine bone. I decided to go with the flow, and make it like a double chop. Sort of like a double rib lamb chop, except much, much bigger. This recipe will work with or without the chine bone.

The only flavoring used in this recipe is the olive oil marinade and the cooking fat. The flavor of bison cooked this way needs no other seasoning.

Serves 2 to 4

1 (2½ to 4 pound) 2-rib bison standing rib roast, bone in

For the Marinade
2 tablespoons unfiltered organic extra virgin olive oil

For Pre-Browning
2 tablespoons beef tallow, (or pastured butter)

1. Rub the olive oil onto all surfaces of the meat at least 2½ hours before you plan to cook it. Let it rest for 2 hours at room temperature.

2. Heat the tallow (or butter) over medium heat in a cast iron frying pan. When the fat is hot and slightly smoking, place the roast meat side down, and cook for 5 minutes. Turn it so the other meat side is down, and cook for 5 more minutes. Brown all the other surfaces of the roast, which should take 1 or 2 minutes on each surface.

3. Remove the meat from the pan. Let it rest, bone side down, on a plate for about 30 minutes.

4. Preheat the oven to 250 degrees. Place the roast, bone side down, in a shallow roasting pan. If the roast has a chine bone, (a large flat bone covering the top of the roast), place the chine bone down.

5. Roast for 30 minutes, or until done to your taste. It should be rare in the middle.

6. Let the roast rest in the turned off oven for 5 minutes.

Use a sharp knife to separate the bone from the meat, slice, serve, and experience bison eating heaven.

Bone In Bison Short Loin Roast

It's quite likely that you have never even heard of a bone in short loin roast before, let alone a bison bone in short loin roast. Long ago, the beef version of this cut was quite popular in Britain and the United States. In modern times, the short loin is most commonly cut into steaks, usually boneless.

This will be one of the best meat experiences you have had. If you follow this recipe, and use the right ingredients, you cannot fail.

This is a luxury cut, to be enjoyed and savored. The large proportion of bone gives a deep and wonderful flavor to the meat, while protecting it from drying out. The fat cap bastes the meat as it cooks, imparting a wonderful flavor.

Serves 4

1 (3 to 4 pound) bone in bison short loin roast, with fat cap

For the Marinade
2 tablespoons unfiltered organic extra virgin olive oil
4 cloves organic garlic, chopped

For Roasting
½ teaspoon freshly ground organic black pepper

1. The day before you plan to make the roast, rub the meat sides with the olive oil. Press the garlic into both of the meat sides. Let rest at room temperature for 1 hour, then cover and refrigerate overnight.

2. An hour before you plan to cook the meat, remove it from the refrigerator, so it can come to room temperature.

3. Preheat the oven to 400 degrees. Scrape the garlic off the meat, and sprinkle all over with pepper (including the bones). Place the roast bone side down in a shallow roasting pan. (The bone side is the big flat bone that covers one side of the roast.) Put the roast in the oven, and cook at 400 degrees for 15 minutes.

4. Turn the heat down to 250 degrees. Cook for 30 minutes.

5. Check for doneness. Done in this case means that the center of this roast is rare, about 115 degrees. If the roast is not done, check for doneness at 10 minute intervals.

To carve the roast, place it bone side down on the carving board. Starting at the highest point of the roast, cut between the bones and meat, following the line of the bone. You are going to make one long L-shaped cut which should enable you to remove all the meat from the bone with one cut. Slice, serve, and enjoy.

Royal Bison Roast in the Style of Poland

I was surprised to learn that bison were not confined to North America. The deep Polish forests contain herds of forest bison, a species very closely related to American bison. I was delighted to learn that bison was considered a royal dish in Old Poland, a dish that was literally fit for a king.

This recipe uses traditional Polish flavors, which are carried deep into the meat by the olive oil to create a dish that may or may not be royal, but is absolutely tender and delicious. It is very important to use the leaves of the celery, rather than the stalks. The leaves have a distinct flavor that fits well in this dish.

Serves 4 to 6

1 (2 to 3½ pound) bison sirloin tip roast, trimmed of outside sinew

For the Marinade

2 dried bay leaves, crushed

½ teaspoon freshly ground organic black pepper

1 teaspoon dried organic marjoram, crushed.

2 tablespoons organic celery leaves, finely chopped

1 teaspoon organic onion powder

¼ cup unfiltered organic extra virgin olive oil

1 small organic onion, thinly sliced

For Roasting

Fat, traditionally made bacon, (or thinly sliced pastured butter)

1. The day before you plan to cook the roast, combine the bay leaves, pepper, marjoram, celery leaves, and onion powder. Rub this mixture on all sides of the roast, coating it evenly. Pour the olive oil over the roast, and roll the roast in the oil, making sure that all sides are coated. Place the roast in a bowl just large enough to hold it, and cover it with the onion slices. Let rest for 1 hour at room temperature, then cover and refrigerate overnight.

2. At least 1 hour before you plan to cook the roast, take it out of the refrigerator so it can come to room temperature.

3. Preheat the oven to 400 degrees. Scrape the marinade off the roast, and reserve. Prepare a bed for the roast. To do this, take 2 strips of bacon, cut them in half, and put them in the center of the roasting pan in a square (alternatively you can use several slices of butter). Use the marinade to fill up the square, making a bed for the roast. Put the roast on top of the square. Cover the top of the roast with more bacon slices (or butter slices).

4. Put the roast in the oven, and cook for 15 minutes.

5. Baste the roast with the pan drippings. Turn the heat down to 250 degrees, and cook for 20 minutes. This should give you a roast that is rare in the middle and pink toward the outside. If the roast is not done to your taste, you can continue cooking it at 250 degrees, checking for doneness at 5 minute intervals. Remember, bison cooks quickly.

Serve, slice against the grain, and enjoy the royal flavors and the sweet bison meat.

High-Low Bison Roast

Most modern recipes for bison roasts suggest cooking them in a slow cooker, or at super low heat for a long time. Most older recipes for bison roast insist on larding the meat. Since I don't like the taste or texture of meat cooked in a slow cooker, and since larding is a skill I've never acquired, I decided to see if the time-honored High-Low Method would work on bison. I am happy to report that it does. Even better than expected. Because the bison is so lean, the olive oil marinade and the bacon topping are absolutely necessary. If you do this recipe right, you will be rewarded with a beautifully colored roast that ranges from pink to medium rare on the inside, has a wonderful bison flavor, and is very tender.

Serves 4

1 (2 to 3 pound) bison sirloin tip roast

For the Marinade

¼ cup unfiltered organic extra virgin olive oil

For Roasting

1 medium onion, sliced into 3 circles of roughly even thickness

Fat, traditionally made bacon slices, (or thinly sliced pastured butter)

1. The day before you plan to cook the roast, pour the olive oil over it, making sure that all sides are covered with the olive oil. Place the roast in the smallest bowl that will hold it, and pour the remaining olive oil over the roast. Let the roast rest for 1 hour at room temperature, then cover and refrigerate overnight.

2. At least 1 hour before you plan to cook the roast, remove the roast from the refrigerator, so it can come to room temperature.

3. Preheat the oven to 425 degrees. Arrange the onion slices in the center of a flat roasting pan so they form a bed for the roast. Remove the roast from the marinade. Place the roast on the bed of onions, and cover the roast with the bacon slices. Put the roast in the oven, and cook for 20 minutes.

4. Reduce the heat to 250 degrees, and cook for another 15 minutes.

5. Turn off the oven without opening the door, and cook for another 5 minutes.

6. Test for doneness with a meat thermometer. If the roast is not done to your taste, return to the oven, and test for doneness at 5 minute intervals. Please bear in mind that bison cooks very quickly, and should not be cooked beyond medium rare.

Serve the roast, slice against the grain, and get ready to enjoy some tender, tasty bison.

Tender Roast Bison Shoulder

Can lean meat be tender when roasted? Conventional cooking says no. I say very lean meat can be roasted tender, with an absolutely delicious taste from the meat itself.

This recipe was somewhat of a test. I wanted to roast a piece of very lean meat, and I wanted it to be tender. Bison is very lean. Bison does not have marbling. The shoulder is even leaner. Fortunately, it does not have much connective tissue. Because this meat is so lean, I decided to use all three of the basic tenderizing techniques. These techniques worked! Try this for some tender, delicious roast bison.

Serves 4

1 (2 to 3 pound) bison shoulder roast, silverskin trimmed off

For the Marinade
2 tablespoons unfiltered organic extra virgin olive oil
6 organic green onions, both white and green parts, crushed
4 organic garlic cloves, crushed

For Pre-Browning
2 tablespoons pastured butter, (or melted beef tallow)

1. The night before you plan to make the roast, coat all surfaces with the olive oil. Crush the onions and garlic together, then press the crushed vegetables and any juices into all sides of the meat. Let sit for 1 hour at room temperature, then place in a covered glass bowl, and refrigerate overnight.

2. Take the roast out of the refrigerator at least 2¼ hours before you plan to cook it.

3. Brush the vegetables off the meat, and reserve. Wipe the meat dry.

4. When the meat has come to room temperature (about 1 hour), heat the butter (or tallow) in a cast iron frying pan. When the fat is hot and slightly smoking, brown the roast on all sides. Be careful to avoid scorching the roast while browning it.

5. Let the meat rest on a plate at room temperature for 1 hour.

6. Preheat the oven to 250 degrees. Place the crushed vegetables in the center of a small roasting pan. Place the meat on the vegetables. Roast at 250 degrees for 30 minutes. Test for doneness. If the meat is not done to your taste, continue cooking at 250 degrees, checking for doneness every 5 minutes. This bison roast should be served rare.

Very tender, and so delicious.

Bison Pot Roast in the Style of Ancient Rome

The ancient Romans were both famous and infamous for their obsession with food. Some of the most famous and powerful Romans, including some emperors, took an intense interest in obtaining the most exotic food imaginable, and spent a fortune for rare and hard to get ingredients. The Roman obsession with particular ingredients even led to the extinction of several species of plants. One favorite seasoning used to be silphium. Silphium was a plant that grew in the Libyan desert which became extinct from overharvesting by Roman gourmets. Garlic is probably the closest modern equivalent. Another typical seasoning was garum, which was made from fish, concentrated grape juice, and other ingredients. Garum was used in a huge variety of dishes. The closest modern equivalent is the fish sauce from Asian countries such as Thailand.

Roman epicures also sought exotic animals from far away lands for their feasts. The idea for this recipe came to me after reading about a Roman feast that featured bison cooked with figs. You may be wondering how the Romans could get to the American prairie to snag a bison for their dinner. The bison could only have been the European bison which lived in the great European forest of the time. Even today, there are European bison living in the Polish forest. They look very much like American bison, only smaller.

The Romans believed that cooking meat with figs would make it more tender. Some Roman cookbooks and writings on cooking have survived to the present day. While I did not find a recipe for bison, I did find a number of recipes for roasting and stewing meat. I put this recipe together as a guess as to how the Romans might have cooked bison with figs. Sometimes you get lucky. This recipe came out exotic and delicious on the first try.

Serves 4

1 (2 to 3 pound) bison chuck roast, preferably bone in

For the Marinade

    1 tablespoon fresh organic rosemary leaves, finely chopped

    1 tablespoon fresh organic celery leaves, finely chopped

    2 tablespoons fresh organic Italian parsley leaves, finely chopped

    1 teaspoon fresh organic thyme leaves, finely chopped

    4 organic garlic cloves, finely chopped

    2 teaspoons fresh organic ginger, finely chopped

    1 teaspoon freshly ground organic black pepper

    3 tablespoons unfiltered organic extra virgin olive oil

    1 tablespoon Thai fish sauce

For Pot Roasting

2 to 4 tablespoons extra virgin olive oil

1 medium organic onion, sliced

2 stalks organic celery, sliced

8 dried organic figs, chopped

1½ cup homemade *Beef* or *Bison Broth* (pages 45 - 53)

2 teaspoons arrowroot, mixed with 2 teaspoons filtered water

1. The day before you plan to make the pot roast, combine all the ingredients for the marinade, and mix well. Place the bison in a glass bowl, just large enough to hold it, and rub the marinade into the meat on all sides. Cover and refrigerate overnight.

2. An hour before you plan to start cooking the bison, remove it from the refrigerator.

3. Once the bison has come to room temperature, scrape off the marinade with a spoon, and reserve. Heat 2 tablespoons extra virgin olive oil over medium heat in a large cast iron frying pan, or casserole. Brown the bison gently on all sides. This should take 6 to 10 minutes. Remove the bison from the pan, and let it rest on a plate.

4. Examine the pan drippings. If it looks like you have less than 2 tablespoons of oil, add more oil until you have about 2 tablespoons. Add the onion, celery, and reserved marinade (which is mostly herbs) to the pan. Cook for 10 minutes over medium heat, stirring occasionally. Add the figs, and mix well.

5. Divide the mixture into two equal parts, moving each half to a different side of the pan so you have a clear space in which to place the bison. Place the bison in the pan, and move the vegetables all around it. Add the broth, and bring to a simmer. Cover the pan, and let simmer for 30 minutes.

6. Turn the bison over, cover the pan, and simmer for another 15 minutes. Check for doneness. The bison is done when a fork or skewer goes in easily, and comes out hot to the touch. If the bison is not done, cover, and simmer for another 15 minutes. It should be ready at that point. Remember, bison cooks very quickly. If it is not ready, reduce the heat to a very low simmer, and check for doneness at 10 minute intervals.

7. When the bison is ready, remove the meat from the pan, and let rest in a warm place. Thicken the sauce with the arrowroot mixture until it is thick enough to coat the back of a spoon.

Slice the bison thinly against the grain, and pour the sauce on. Enjoy the exotic flavor.

Bison Pot Roast with Blueberries, European Vegetables, and Potatoes

Blueberries tenderize bison as they cook together. And blueberries go so well with bison. The flavors complement each other perfectly. Add the traditional European vegetable trio of onions, carrots, and celery, and you have something special. Add some homemade broth to bind, blend, and enrich the flavors, and it's even better. Add some potatoes, and you have a one pot meal, with the potatoes soaking up some of the wonderful blueberry spiked broth to become both slightly purple and absolutely delicious.

This is a truly robust and hearty dish, but not at all heavy, thanks to the clean, sweet, lean quality of the bison. Since this is bison, no salt is required.

Serves 4

1 (2 to 3 pound) bison roast, either sirloin tip, rump, or chuck

For Pre-Browning

2 tablespoons pastured butter

For Pot Roasting

1 medium organic onion, coarsely chopped

2 stalks organic celery, (interior stalks with some leaves), coarsely chopped

3 large carrots, coarsely chopped

3 medium potatoes, peeled and cut into 1 inch cubes

1 cup organic or wild blueberries, fresh or frozen, (thawed if frozen)

2 cups good homemade broth, such as *Bison* or *Nomad's Broth* (pages 45 - 53)

1 to 2 tablespoons pastured butter, softened

1. At least 2 hours before you plan to cook the roast, trim any membranes from the roast (save them for a future broth). Dry the roast. In a heavy bottomed pan, heat 2 tablespoons of butter over medium heat until hot and slightly smoking. Brown the roast on all sides until it is a light to medium brown color. Do not let it scorch. When the roast is browned, remove it from the heat, and let it rest for at least 2 hours. (The roast will be even more tender if you brown it the day before, let it cool for 1 hour, then cover and refrigerate overnight.)

2. If the roast was refrigerated, remove it from the refrigerator 1 hour before you plan to cook it, so it can come to room temperature.

3. Mix the chopped onion, celery, and carrots together. Rub 1 to 2 tablespoons of softened butter all over the inside of a cast iron casserole. Cover the bottom of the casserole with some of the vegetable mixture. Place the roast on the vegetables. Add the potatoes and blueberries to the rest of the vegetable mixture, and surround the roast with it. Pour the broth over all.

4. Preheat the oven to 250 degrees. Place the pot on the stove over medium heat, and bring to a simmer, reducing the heat once a simmer is reached. Once the contents of the pot have reached a strong simmer, cover, and place it in the preheated oven.

5. Cook for 1½ to 2 hours, or until the meat is easily pierced with a fork.

Serve, slice against the grain, and enjoy this wonderful pot roast.

Bison Pot Roast

Grassfed bison is even leaner than grassfed beef. The European cooks who invented pot roast recognized the need to add fat to lean meat to make it tender and delicious. One of their methods was to use an oil-based marinade. This marinade is adapted from several European marinades, and it works beautifully with bison. This marinade also brings out the wonderful natural flavor of grassfed bison.

Serves 4

1 (2 to 3 pound) bison sirloin tip roast

For the Marinade

4 tablespoons unfiltered organic extra virgin olive oil

1 medium organic carrot, peeled and chopped into small pieces, and crushed

1 medium onion, finely chopped and crushed

2 organic garlic cloves, peeled and finely chopped, and crushed

4 sprigs organic Italian parsley, finely chopped, and crushed

1 dried bay leaf, crushed and crumbled

¼ teaspoon organic dried thyme

½ teaspoon freshly ground organic black pepper

For Pot Roasting

2 tablespoons pastured butter

1 large organic onion, peeled and sliced

4 medium sized organic carrots, peeled and chopped

½ bunch organic Italian parsley, with stems, finely chopped

6 small organic potatoes, peeled and quartered

2 cups good homemade broth, such as *Bison Broth* (page 46)

1 tablespoon arrowroot, mixed with 1 tablespoon filtered water

1. Combine the ingredients for the marinade, and mix well. Place the roast in a bowl that is just a little bigger than the roast. Add the well-mixed marinade, and turn the roast to make sure that all sides are coated with the marinade. Let sit at room temperature for 1 hour, then cover and refrigerate overnight.

2. Take the roast out of the refrigerator at least 1 hour before you plan to cook it, so it can come to room temperature.

3. After the roast has reached room temperature, remove it from the marinade. Reserve the marinade. Preheat the oven to 300 degrees.

4. Melt the butter in a cast iron casserole over medium heat. When the butter is hot and slightly smoking, brown the roast on all sides, turning frequently, taking care not to scorch it. When the roast has been browned, remove it from the pot, and let it rest on a plate. Add the onions, carrots, and parsley to the drippings, and sauté over medium heat for 5 minutes, until the vegetables are lightly colored and reduced in volume.

5. Remove the vegetables from the reserved marinade with a slotted spoon, and add to the pot. Add the roast to the pot, and place it in the middle of the vegetables. Add the broth. Add the potatoes, placing them around the roast, and pushing them under the broth. Bring the broth to a simmer. Cover the pot, and put it in the oven at 300 degrees. Let it cook for 1 hour, then test for doneness by sticking a large fork or skewer into the meat. If it goes in easily, the meat is ready. If not, return the meat to the oven, cover, and check for doneness at 10 minute intervals. Remember that bison cooks even faster than other grassfed meat.

6. When the roast is ready, remove it, and place it on a plate in a warm place. Put the uncovered pot on the stove, and bring the broth to a simmer. Add the arrowroot mixture, stir well, and simmer until the broth has thickened. Remove the potatoes with a slotted spoon, and place in a bowl for serving.

You should have a wonderful, thick gravy loaded with little pieces of cooked down, soft vegetables, including little fragments of potato. This mixture is one of the tastiest, healthiest elixirs you will ever eat. Only a barbarian would strain it. Serve, slice against the grain, and enjoy.

Blueberry Bison Stew

Bison was the most important food of the Native Americans who lived on the Great Plains. Some traditional recipes have been passed down. While there is a wide variety in ingredients, the use of blueberries in bison stews is very common. This recipe shows that the people who lived on bison knew how to cook it. The blueberries make the meat more tender, and blend perfectly with the green onions and broth to make a wonderful sauce. The potatoes absorb some of the sauce, and go wonderfully with everything else. As always, bison is very lean, so it is important to add the fat contained in the recipe. Traditionally, many Native Americans cooked bison without salt, and we have followed this tradition. While it may seem unusual to add berries to a stew, it tastes great.

Serves 4

1½ to 2 pounds bison stew meat, cut into 1 inch cubes

3 tablespoons bison fat, (or beef tallow, bacon drippings, or pastured butter)

1 bunch organic green onions, chopped small

1 cup wild blueberries, fresh or frozen, (thawed if frozen)

1 cup good natural broth, such as *Beef* or *Bison Broth* (pages 45 - 53)

2 large potatoes, peeled and cut into 1 inch cubes

1. Melt the fat over medium heat in a cast iron casserole. When the fat is hot and slightly smoking, put the bison cubes in the pot, and stir until the cubes are lightly browned on all sides.

2. Remove the bison from the casserole. Put the green onions in the pot, and cook for 5 minutes over medium heat, stirring occasionally.

3. Return the bison to the casserole. Add the blueberries, broth, and potatoes, and mix well. Turn the heat down to low, cover, and simmer for 1 to 2 hours, or until the bison is tender. It is important that it simmers, and does not boil. Check how the meat is cooking, and adjust the heat as necessary to keep the stew at a simmer.

Serve and enjoy.

Delicious Bison Burger

Bison is very lean. A few simple steps will tenderize ground bison, and give you absolutely delicious bison burgers. The addition of a little unfiltered extra virgin olive oil makes a big difference. It is also important to have the meat at room temperature before cooking, and to use no salt.

If you like your bison burgers medium, the meat should be formed into patties about ½ inch thick. It you like them medium rare to rare (my favorite), form the meat into 1 inch thick patties. These burgers are so good that they need no cheese, or anything else.

Serves 4

1 pound ground bison

For the Marinade
1 tablespoon unfiltered organic extra virgin olive oil

For Sautéing
2 tablespoons pastured butter

1. Mix the olive oil into the bison about 1 hour before you plan to cook it. Let rest at room temperature.

2. Melt the butter in a cast iron frying pan over medium heat until hot and slightly smoking.

3. Sauté the burgers for 2 to 3 minutes on each side, depending on the thickness of the patty, and how you like them done.

Serve and enjoy.

Tender
Grassfed Lamb

Quick Chops

These chops are very quick to cook, though they're best if marinated first. Grassfed lamb really benefits from a good marinade, which is why there are so many excellent traditional marinades for lamb. The marinade for these chops uses a combination of French and Spanish flavors, which works beautifully together. These little chops cook quickly, and taste great.

Serves 4

8 small-rib lamb chops, with most of the fat trimmed off

For the Marinade
2 cloves organic garlic, peeled

1 tablespoon fresh organic thyme leaves

2 tablespoons fresh organic parsley

¼ teaspoon coarse unrefined sea salt, crushed

1 teaspoon freshly ground organic black pepper

3 tablespoons unfiltered organic extra virgin olive oil

For Sautéing
2 tablespoons organic extra virgin olive oil

1. Place the garlic, thyme, and parsley on a cutting board, and chop them together until they are finely chopped. Mix in a small bowl with the salt, pepper, and unfiltered extra virgin olive oil. Rub this marinade all over the chops, making sure that each chop is well coated. Marinate the lamb chops in this mixture at room temperature for up to 1 hour. (15 minutes would be enough, but a longer time will result in a more intense flavor.)

2. Brush the marinade off the chops.

3. Heat the olive oil in a cast iron frying pan over medium heat. When the oil is hot, add the chops and sauté for 1 to 3 minutes on each side, depending on how well done you like the chops.

This should give you beautiful chops that are crusty on the outside, and juicy on the inside. Be sure to serve hot.

Italian Style Lamb Chops

Loin lamb chops are the Porterhouse of lamb. The bone gives them an incredible flavor. A good marinade only improves the flavor. The marinade we use here is very Italian in concept, very simple, and very delicious.

Serves 4

2 pounds loin lamb chops, bone in, 1 to 1½ inches thick
2 tablespoons white wine, such as sherry

For the Marinade
2 tablespoons unfiltered organic extra virgin olive oil
4 cloves organic garlic, finely chopped
Leaves from 2 branches of organic fresh rosemary, finely chopped
1 teaspoon coarse unrefined sea salt, crushed
1 teaspoon freshly ground organic black pepper

For Cooking
2 tablespoons organic extra virgin olive oil

1. Rub the white wine into the chops on all sides.

2. Combine the unfiltered olive oil, garlic, rosemary, salt and pepper to make a marinade. Mix well. Rub this marinade all over the chops. Let sit at room temperature for about 1 hour before cooking.

3. Heat a large cast iron frying pan over medium heat. Coat lightly with olive oil. Put the chops in the frying pan, and cook for 3 to 5 minutes on each side, depending on how rare you want them to be.

Serve hot, and enjoy.

Transylvanian Lamb Chops

Transylvania has become infamous as the home of Dracula, a vampire that could be repelled by garlic. In cooking terms, this means that any dish called "Transylvanian" must have garlic in it. However, there's a lot more to Transylvanian cooking than garlic. The real Transylvania, which is located between Hungary and Romania and is claimed by both (most of it is part of Romania now), has a remarkable and sophisticated cuisine. The marinade combines flavors that have been traditionally used in Transylvania, plus garlic. It really brings out the flavor of grassfed lamb.

Serves 4

8 loin lamb chops, no more than 1 inch thick

For the Marinade
1 teaspoon sweet paprika

1 teaspoon coarse unrefined sea salt, crushed

1 teaspoon organic garlic powder

½ teaspoon organic mustard powder

½ teaspoon organic powdered ginger

¼ teaspoon organic dried thyme, crushed between your fingers

2 tablespoons unfiltered organic extra virgin olive oil

For Cooking
2 tablespoons extra virgin olive oil

1. Combine all ingredients for the marinade, and mix well. Rub the marinade into the chops. Let the chops marinate at room temperature for 1 hour.

2. Heat the olive oil in a cast iron frying pan over medium high heat. When the oil is hot, cook the chops for 3 minutes on each side, (2 minutes on each side if they are thinner chops).

Serve hot.

Herb Roasted Rack of Lamb

For thousands of years in the Mediterranean, lamb has been roasted with fresh herbs. The wood of the herbs was placed on the fire, and the leaves were rubbed into the meat, often with olive oil. It was thought that the aromatic essences of the roasting herbs pleased the gods. It is certain that these aromas penetrated the meat, enhancing its flavor, and imparting a distinctive taste. This lamb roast uses some of the ancient herbs in a similar way. The leaves are rubbed into the meat with olive oil, and the woody stems are placed directly on the roasting pan under the meat. We use no garlic in this recipe, so the flavor of the herbs really comes through without competition. Those ancients were on to something.

Serves 2

1 rack of lamb, approximately 1½ pounds

For the Marinade
2 sprigs fresh organic rosemary
8 sprigs fresh organic thyme
4 sprigs fresh organic oregano
4 leafy sprigs fresh organic Italian parsley
2 tablespoons unfiltered organic extra virgin olive oil

1. At least 2 hours before you plan to cook the rack, remove the leaves from all the herbs, and reserve the stems. Mix all the leaves together, and chop them finely. Mix the herbs with the olive oil, and rub the mixture all over the rack of lamb, especially on the meaty surfaces. Place the rack in a bowl, and let rest 2 hours at room temperature. (Or let rest for 1 hour at room temperature, cover, and refrigerate overnight.)

2. If the lamb was refrigerated, take it out of the refrigerator about 1 hour before cooking, so it can come to room temperature.

3. Preheat the oven to 425 degrees. Place the stems together in the middle of a roasting pan. Place the rack of lamb, bone side down, directly over the stems. Roast for 25 to 35 minutes, depending on how well done you like the meat.

Serve hot, and enjoy the ancient flavors.

Rack of Lamb with the Flavors of Spain

Lamb has long been appreciated in Spain. There are many excellent recipes. This recipe combines the traditional flavors of truffles, olive oil, garlic, thyme, rosemary, parsley, and paprika to make an almost magical combination, infusing the lamb with intense flavors that result in a superb piece of meat. Pre-salting grassfed lamb does not toughen the meat.

Serves 2

1 rack of lamb, approximately 1½ pounds

For the Marinade

2 tablespoons truffle oil (see note below)

2 tablespoons sherry (preferably Spanish)

½ teaspoon coarse sea salt, crushed

1 tablespoon fresh organic Italian parsley, finely chopped

1 tablespoon fresh organic rosemary leaves, chopped

2 teaspoons fresh organic thyme leaves, chopped

½ teaspoon Spanish sweet (dulce) paprika

½ teaspoon freshly ground organic black pepper

For Cooking

1 organic onion, cut into 3 equal circles

1. At least 2 hours before you plan to cook the lamb, make the marinade. It will be even better if you can marinate it overnight. Combine the marinade ingredients, and mix well. Rub all over the lamb. Let marinate 2 hours at room temperature. (Or let rest for 1 hour at room temperature, cover, and refrigerate overnight.)

2. If the lamb was refrigerated, take it out of the refrigerator about 1 hour before cooking, so it can come to room temperature.

3. Preheat the oven to 425 degrees.

4. Place the onion slices in a row in the center of a roasting pan. Place the rack, bone side down, on the onion slices. (The rack should be fat side up.)

5. Cook for 25 minutes. This should give you a rack of lamb that is medium to medium rare.

Serve hot. Absolutely delicious.

NOTE: You can use extra virgin olive oil (preferably Spanish), if truffle oil is not available.

Castilian Lamb Rack with Chine

Rack of lamb is a luxury roast in any cuisine. This recipe is intended for the most natural way to trim a rack of lamb, a rack which has all of its bones, including the chine bone, and some fat cap. You may not have seen a complete chine bone. A chine bone covers the meat of the rack up to the point where the bone joins with the fat. A roast like this is completely enclosed in bone and fat, except for the meat visible on each end. The cooking time for a rack of lamb with chine is quite different than for one without a chine bone. The bone protects the meat during the roasting process, and gives it great flavor and juiciness.

It is traditional in Castile to grill lamb chops with fresh rosemary and thyme sprigs thrown into the fire. The herbs impart a wonderful flavor to the meat as they burn and smoke. I decided to incorporate these flavors in a different way, to great success.

Don't be intimidated by the task of carving the roast. While you can't cut it into chops, you can slice where the bones join the meat, free the meat from the bones, and remove it in one cylindrical piece, which you can easily slice.

Serves 2 to 3

1 (1½ to 2½ pound) rack of lamb with all of the chine bone, the bones should not be cracked

1 tablespoon fresh organic rosemary leaves

1 tablespoon fresh organic thyme leaves

2 cloves organic garlic, peeled

2 tablespoons unfiltered organic extra virgin olive oil, preferably Spanish

1. Remove the roast from the refrigerator 1 hour before you plan to cook it, so it can come to room temperature.

2. Finely chop the rosemary, thyme, and garlic together. Chopping them together will combine their flavors. When they have been finely chopped, combine them with the olive oil. Rub this mixture all over the rack of lamb, including the fat and the bones.

3. Preheat the oven to 425 degrees.

4. Place the rack in a small roasting pan, and put it in the oven. Cook 25 minutes for rare, and 30 minutes for medium to medium rare.

Serve hot, and enjoy the succulence that only a bone in roast can have.

High-Low Marinated Lamb

Marinating lamb with traditional ingredients can really improve its flavor. This recipe uses both fresh and dried thyme. Using the thyme in two different forms provides a greater depth of flavor.

You can use salt in a recipe for grassfed lamb without worrying that it will toughen the meat, because it won't.

Serves 4

1 (2-pound) boneless leg of lamb, with fat cap. (For a 4-pound leg of lamb, double the ingredients.)

For the Marinade

4 cloves organic garlic, finely chopped

2 tablespoons fresh organic lemon juice

2 tablespoons unfiltered organic extra virgin olive oil

1 teaspoon coarse unrefined sea salt, crushed

1 teaspoon fresh organic thyme leaves

½ teaspoon dried organic thyme leaves, preferably wild

½ teaspoon freshly ground organic black pepper

For the Vegetable Rack

1 organic carrot, peeled, and cut into 6 or 7 pieces

1 organic onion, medium size, cut into 4 circles of equal thickness

1. Mix all the marinade ingredients until they are well blended. Rub the marinade into the lamb. Place the lamb and the marinade in a covered glass bowl just large enough to hold the lamb. Refrigerate for 1 to 2 days, being sure to turn the lamb over in the marinade at least once a day.

2. Remove the lamb from the refrigerator about 2 hours before you plan to cook it.

3. Form a bed for the lamb with the carrot pieces and onions, about the size of the lamb. Place the lamb directly on the vegetables.

4. Preheat the oven to 425 degrees. Place the lamb in the oven, and cook for 15 minutes. Remove the lamb from the oven, baste, and return to the oven for another 15 minutes.

5. Remove the lamb from the oven, baste with the pan drippings, return the lamb to the oven, and reduce the heat to 300 degrees. Cook for 15 minutes.

6. Turn the heat down to 225 degrees, and cook for 10 minutes. This should give you a tender piece of lamb that is slightly pink in the middle, juicy, and savory with all the flavors of the marinade. If the lamb is not done to your taste, you can return it to the oven, and check for doneness in 10 minute intervals.

Serve hot and enjoy.

Roast Leg of Lamb on a Bed of Apples

Roasting apples with meat has delicious results. Some of the juices given off by the roasting apples turn to steam, which permeates the roasting meat with a wonderful flavor. The apples themselves will caramelize, which concentrates their flavor deliciously. Be careful, if you cook the apples too long, they will dry out.

While apples are often roasted with pork, here we roast them with lamb. We keep them from drying out by roasting them under a boneless leg of lamb, which gives great flavor to the meat, while protecting the apples. The garlic and rosemary complement the sweetness of the apples perfectly.

Serves 4 to 6

1 (3 to 5 pound) boneless leg of lamb, with some fat, unrolled and laid flat

2 tablespoons unfiltered organic apple cider vinegar

2 large cloves organic garlic, quartered lengthwise

Leaves from 1 large sprig fresh organic rosemary

1 teaspoon coarse unrefined sea salt, crushed

1 teaspoon freshly ground organic black pepper

2 large organic apples, (such as fuji), cored and quartered

1. Rub the vinegar all over the lamb.

2. Cut 8 slits into the fat side of the lamb. Place one garlic quarter in each slit, with a few rosemary leaves. Rub the salt and pepper over the lamb.

3. Preheat the oven to 425 degrees. Place the apple quarters, skin side down, in the center of a large roasting pan. Place the lamb, fat side up, on the apples.

4. Cook for 15 minutes.

5. Baste the lamb with the pan juices, reduce the heat to 300 degrees, and cook for 1 hour for pink meat. Cook 10 to 20 minutes longer if you want the meat more well done.

Be sure to serve the delicious apples with the lamb.

Roast Leg of Lamb with Herbs
in the Style of Castile

Spain is famous for its magnificent roast lamb. This is especially true in the region of Castile, which has an honored tradition of preparing some of the best roast lamb on the planet. It is impossible to fully recreate the taste of Castilian roast lamb in America, unless you could import very young lamb directly from Castile. This is true because the taste of lamb is so dependent on what the lamb eats, and on the size and age of the lamb. Spanish sheep and lambs often graze on pasture that is rich with wild herbs, which impart a wonderful taste to the meat. Even if the lamb is so young that it is almost totally milk fed, the milk would be heavily flavored by the herbs. The best lambs are very young and very small when they are processed. Spanish lambs are so tender that they are traditionally carved with the edge of a plate. They are roasted simply, with few seasonings. Even the best American grassfed lambs do not eat those wild herbs, and are not processed at such an early age.

This recipe is based on the principle that if the herbs are not in the meat, bring the herbs to the meat. I use some of the same herbs that grow wild in Spain. I also use the smallest lamb legs I can find. Here, 4¼ pounds is tiny. I do use salt and wine in this marinade, as they will not toughen lamb, especially if there is enough oil in the marinade. The extensive use of fresh herbs, along with other flavors, will turn any leg of lamb into a magnificent feast. While you will need more than a plate to carve this roast, it is wonderfully tender.

Serves 4 to 6

1 (4 to 5 pound) leg of lamb, bone in, with some fat cap
2 cloves organic garlic, quartered lengthwise

For the Marinade

8 sprigs fresh organic thyme
8 sprigs fresh organic oregano
2 sprigs fresh organic rosemary
Leaves from 4 sprigs fresh organic parsley
4 cloves organic garlic, finely chopped
¼ cup unfiltered organic extra virgin olive oil, preferably Spanish
2 tablespoons sherry, preferably Spanish

For the Spice Rub

1 teaspoon coarse unrefined sea salt, crushed
½ teaspoon freshly ground organic black pepper
¼ teaspoon sweet Spanish paprika

1. Begin marinating the lamb at least 3 hours before you start cooking it. Cut 8 deep slits all over the top of the lamb. Push a garlic sliver into each slit.

2. Strip the leaves from all of the thyme and oregano sprigs, and from one of the sprigs of rosemary. Reserve the stripped stems and the other sprig of rosemary. Chop the herb and parsley leaves together with the garlic, until finely chopped. Place in a small bowl with the olive oil and wine, and mix well to make a marinade. Mix the salt, pepper, and paprika, and rub all over the meat. Place the leg in a glass container large enough to hold it, and rub the marinade all over the lamb. Let rest at a cool room temperature for 3 hours.

3. Preheat the oven to 425 degrees. Place the reserved rosemary sprig and the stripped stems in a well-greased roasting pan. Place the meaty bottom of the roast over the sprigs. Pour any marinade still in the container over the roast. Roast for 15 minutes.

4. Baste the roast with the pan drippings. Reduce the heat to 300 degrees, and cook for 30 minutes.

5. Baste the roast with the pan drippings, and cook for another 30 minutes. This should give you a roast that is pink to light grey, juicy, tender, and delicious.

Roast Lamb Shoulder with Greek Flavors

The Greeks have enjoyed roast lamb for thousands of years. Throughout that long tradition, they have always used local herbs to flavor it, along with their excellent olive oil. The herbs really improve the flavor of the lamb. This version uses both fresh and dried oregano, which creates a deep, rich flavor. While it is traditional to roast the lamb in front of a fire, the oven works just fine. Try to use Greek olive oil if you can get it. It really makes a difference. The meat should be cooked to medium.

Serves 4 to 6

1 (2 to 4 pound) bone in lamb shoulder, (or arm roast)
4 organic garlic cloves, halved lengthwise

For the Marinade

3 tablespoons unfiltered organic extra virgin olive oil, preferably Greek
1 tablespoon fresh organic lemon juice
1 teaspoon coarse unrefined sea salt, crushed
½ teaspoon freshly ground organic black pepper
1 teaspoon dried organic oregano
4 sprigs fresh organic oregano, coarsely chopped
2 sprigs fresh organic rosemary, coarsely chopped
2 sprigs fresh organic thyme, coarsely chopped

1. The day before you plan to cook the roast, cut eight slits into the meat, and insert a halved garlic clove in each one. Place the meat in a glass bowl. Combine the marinade ingredients, mix well, and rub all over the meat. Let sit for 1 hour at room temperature, then cover and refrigerate overnight.

2. Take the meat out of the refrigerator 1 hour before you plan to cook it, so it can come to room temperature.

3. Preheat the oven to 425 degrees.

4. Place the roast in the center of a roasting pan. Place the pan in the center of the oven. Cook for 10 minutes. Baste the roast, then cook for another 10 minutes.

5. Turn the heat down to 250 degrees, and cook for 30 minutes. Check for doneness. A bigger roast could take another 20 to 30 minutes.

Serve hot, and enjoy the great flavors of Greece.

Roast Lamb with Mediterranean Herbs

Lamb has been the favorite meat in the Mediterranean for thousands of years. It was usually roasted with a variety of herbs native to the Mediterranean, such as thyme, rosemary, sage, and oregano. In this recipe, we use all of these herbs, both in their fresh and dried form. The use of fresh and dried herbs together in the same dish, creates a big flavor that enhances the taste of the tender lamb. The olive oil really brings the flavor of the herbs into the meat.

Rubbing the lamb with the vinegar seems to open the meat even further to the flavor of the herbs.

Serves 4

1 (3 to 5 pound) bone in lamb shoulder
2 tablespoons organic raw unfiltered apple cider vinegar

For the Marinade

1 tablespoon fresh organic thyme leaves, chopped
1 tablespoon fresh organic rosemary leaves, chopped
1 tablespoon fresh organic sage leaves, chopped
1 tablespoon fresh organic oregano leaves, chopped
¼ teaspoon dried organic thyme, crushed
¼ teaspoon dried organic rosemary crushed
½ teaspoon dried organic sage, crushed
½ teaspoon dried organic oregano, crushed
1 teaspoon coarse unrefined sea salt, crushed
¼ cup unfiltered organic extra virgin olive oil

For Roasting

3 slices fat, traditionally made bacon, (or 3 tablespoons thinly sliced butter)

1. The day before you plan to cook the roast, combine the herbs and salt with the olive oil, mix well. Rub the vinegar all over the lamb, then drain. Rub the olive oil mixture all over the lamb, covering it evenly. Place the lamb and any remaining marinade into a glass bowl just large enough to hold the lamb. Let sit for 1 hour, cover, and refrigerate overnight.

2. Take the lamb out of the refrigerator 1 hour before you plan to cook it, so it can come to room temperature.

3. Preheat the oven to 425 degrees.

4. Place the lamb in the middle of a greased roasting pan. Cover the top of the lamb with bacon (or butter). Put in the preheated oven, and cook for 15 minutes.

5. Turn the heat down to 300 degrees, and cook for 1 hour. The lamb should be tender, medium to pink, and absolutely succulent and delicious.

Serve hot, and enjoy.

Lamburger

Americans usually don't think of lamb when they think of burgers. However, ground lamb has an honored place in the cuisines of many nations. This recipe uses traditional seasonings for lamb, plus the American tradition of the cheeseburger. Even people who think they don't like lamb will enjoy the delicious flavor of the lamburger.

Serves 4

1 pound ground lamb
1 tablespoon extra virgin olive oil
¼ teaspoon dried organic rosemary, crushed
¼ teaspoon dried organic oregano, crushed
¼ teaspoon dried organic thyme, crushed
1 teaspoon dried organic parsley, crushed
½ teaspoon garlic powder

For Sautéing
2 tablespoons pastured butter
4 slices of good natural cheese, Havarti is excellent
4 organic hamburger buns

1. Mix the olive oil, herbs, and garlic powder. Rub the mixture into the ground lamb. Form into 4 equal patties, approximately ½ inch thick, shaped to fit the hamburger buns.

2. Heat the butter over medium heat in a cast iron frying pan. When the butter is hot and slightly smoking, put in the patties, and cook for 3 minutes on one side. Remove the patties from the heat, and carefully pour off most of the fat, leaving just enough to coat the frying pan.

3. Return the pan to the stove, then put the patties back in the pan uncooked side down. Continue to cook over medium heat for 3 minutes. This will give you a burger that is pink and juicy inside. You can cook it longer if you want.

4. Place a slice of cheese over each patty. Turn off the heat. Once the cheese has melted, put each patty on a hamburger bun. Cover the patty with the second half of the bun, and you have a lamburger.

Eat and enjoy.

Basic Lamb Curry

We like this dish so much that we always roast more lamb than we need, so we can make the leftovers into this tasty, spicy, health-giving curry. Curry is a combination of spices that is traditional in Indian cuisine. Many of the ingredients are dried and powdered herbs that have documented healing properties, such as turmeric, cinnamon, cloves, garlic, ginger, and hot peppers. I believe these spice combinations were invented as a way to purify food and promote health. While curry powders are best made from scratch, there are some excellent premixed organic curry powders. This recipe adds a few more ingredients to create a flavor that is very spicy, hot, and thoroughly delicious. The bone broth really unites the flavors. This is a great way to turn leftovers into something special.

Serves 4

2 pounds leftover lamb, cut into 1 inch cubes

2 tablespoons pastured butter

1 large organic onion, sliced

4 cloves organic garlic, crushed

1 (1 inch) piece organic ginger, finely chopped

2 tablespoons organic curry powder

1 teaspoon organic turmeric

1 teaspoon freshly ground organic black pepper

1 teaspoon thick organic hot sauce

1½ cups good homemade broth, such as Chicken or Lamb Broth (pages 45 - 53)

1. Melt the butter over medium heat in a heavy bottomed pan large enough to hold the lamb. When the butter is hot and slightly smoking, add the onions, garlic, and ginger. Cook over medium heat until the onions are soft.

2. Add the curry powder, turmeric, and black pepper to the onions. Reduce the heat to low. Cook for another 5 minutes, stirring the spices into the onions.

3. Add the meat, hot sauce, and bone broth. Mix well. Cover, and simmer for 30 minutes.

Serve and enjoy.

Sneaky Healthy Foods:

How to Eat Liver and Love It!

Finding Grassfed Innard and Liver Sausage

Parents have been trying to get their children to eat innards, such as liver, for hundreds of years. Traditional peoples valued organ meats above all others. Organ meats are full of nutrients, much more so than other meats. Organ meats from grassfed and grass finished animals are very nutritious.

A well made sausage is the easiest way to ingest grassfed organs. Many find the natural texture of liver, kidney, heart, etc. to be unappealing. Sausage has the additional benefit of being a fermented food, which increases certain nutrients. However, most sausages are full of filler ingredients such as soy, powdered milk, and flavoring ingredients such as MSG in its myriad forms, and various sweeteners, not to mention all kinds of preservatives. I would not touch the typical sausage, let alone eat it.

The ideal healthy organ sausage would be made completely from grassfed meats, organs, and fats, with natural spices and casings. Such a sausage would not contain preservatives, soy or other filler materials, MSG or artificial flavorings, or any sweeteners except for the most natural and healthy, such as real honey.

So far, I have only found such sausages at U.S. Wellness Meats (see **Sources** on page 217). They sell liverwurst, braunschweiger, and headcheese that are full of healthy grassfed organ meats, and meet all my other requirements. These sausages work well in my recipes, and are delicious on their own.

Beef Liver Pancake

The health-giving qualities of innards such as liver, heart, and kidneys have been known since ancient Roman times. Unfortunately, these healthy foods are difficult to work with in their raw state, requiring a lot of cutting and trimming. The texture of these organ meats can be unpleasant to many people. These problems have existed since before ancient Roman times. This means that talented cooks have had thousands of years to come up with ways to make liver, heart, and kidneys palatable. One of the best ways was to make these items into sausages, which eliminated the problems with preparation and texture. However, while the strong flavor could be diluted by spices and smoking, it was still too much for many people. An excellent solution to this problem has been to mix the sausage with enough other ingredients to modify the taste to the point where it is actually good. Traditional European cooking is full of recipes for pancakes, dumplings, meatloaf, and other such mixtures utilizing innards. This pancake is delicious as well as healthy. It is based on an excellent sausage made with grassfed beef and grassfed beef liver.

Serves 4

½ pound grassfed beef liver sausage, such as U.S. Wellness braunschweiger

4 slices all natural sourdough bread

1 cup organic whole milk

2 organic eggs

1 teaspoon organic onion powder

1 teaspoon organic garlic powder

½ teaspoon freshly ground organic black pepper

For Cooking

4 tablespoons pastured butter, divided into 2 equal portions

1. Use a blender to reduce the bread to bread crumbs. Soak the bread crumbs in the milk, mixing well. Remove the casing from the sausage, and crumble the sausage with your hands until it is broken up.

2. Beat the eggs until they are bubbly. Mix all the ingredients (except the butter) together in a large bowl, mixing well. On a floured board, form into a big flat pancake. Let rest for 10 minutes.

3. Heat 2 tablespoons of the butter in a cast iron frying pan over medium heat. When the butter is hot and bubbly, carefully place the pancake in the frying pan. Flatten it with the back of a spatula until it covers the entire surface of the frying pan. Cook for 5 minutes.

4. Carefully raise the pancake, add the remaining butter, and turn the pancake over. Cook for another 5 minutes over medium heat.

Serve and enjoy.

Mysterious Russian Hamburgers

Russia has a reputation for mystery, intrigue, and secrets, going back to the Cold War. There is a mystery even in this recipe.

Russian hamburgers are known as kotlety. There are many different kinds. They are a favorite in Russia. However, none of the ones I know about have the mystery ingredient that makes this version so special. I suppose that I can't give you the recipe without disclosing the mystery ingredient, so I must admit that it is — beef liver sausage! It is crumbled and mixed into the meat. Even the most suspicious child will be unable to detect its presence. The spices in the liver sausage really enhance the flavor of this dish.

Serves 4

For the Patties

1 pound grassfed ground beef

¼ pound grassfed liver sausage, such as U.S. Wellness braunschweiger, casings removed, crumbled

1 slice all natural sourdough bread

1 large organic egg

1½ teaspoons organic mustard with seeds

½ teaspoon freshly ground organic black pepper

For Cooking

2 tablespoons pastured butter

1. Use a blender to reduce the bread to bread crumbs.

2. Combine the ingredients for the patties. Mix well. Form into patties about ½ inch thick.

3. Heat the butter over medium heat in a large cast iron frying pan. When the butter is hot and bubbly, cook the patties until golden brown on both sides. About 2 minutes per side should do.

Serve and enjoy the great taste. You need not disclose the mystery ingredient.

Meatloaf with Secret Ingredient

The secret ingredient is the key to the great taste and rejuvenative qualities of this meatloaf. After much research, I am convinced that the internal organs of grassfed animals are extremely nutritious and healthy to eat. As a cook, I must admit that substances such as liver, heart, kidney, etc. are difficult to work with. Truth be told, they are slimy, slippery, and squishy in their raw state. Even worse, these slippery organs usually come complete with all sorts of parts that have to be removed, and seem to have been invented only for the purpose of tormenting cooks. All of which does not change the fact that these organ meats are very nutritious.

It was Sally Fallon who came up with the great idea of using organ sausages in meatloaf. U.S. Wellness has developed some excellent organ sausages, (see **Sources** on page 217). This recipe was created to make use of this wonderful sausage. The results were much tastier than I could have imagined. Even my teenage son liked it.

Serves 4

1 pound grassfed ground beef

¼ pound grassfed organ sausage, such as liverwurst

2 slices all natural sourdough bread

1 large organic onion, finely chopped

2 organic eggs, beaten with a fork

1 teaspoon organic seasoning salt

1 teaspoon sweet Spanish paprika, (or organic paprika)

2 tablespoons pastured butter, cut into tiny cubes

½ cup organic cream

1. Use a blender to reduce the bread to bread crumbs.

2. Preheat the oven to 400 degrees. Place all the ingredients in a large bowl. Mix well with your hands, trying to make sure that all ingredients are mixed evenly together. Once all the ingredients have been mixed evenly together, form into the shape of a loaf.

3. Place the loaf in the middle of a greased glass loaf pan. Bake for 30 minutes, or until the top is firm. This should give you a juicy meatloaf.

Serve and enjoy.

German Style Meatloaf

This recipe is full of liver and it tastes great! This is the first dish containing liver in any form that my teenage son ever liked. The traditional German recipes use two kinds of pork sausages and bacon. This recipe uses grassfed beef organ sausage and butter, because I think they are healthier and tastier. I have made other adjustments as well. The result is so good that even liver haters will enjoy it.

Serves 4

½ pound grassfed organ sausage, such as liverwurst

3 tablespoons pastured butter

1 medium organic onion, finely chopped

1 teaspoon organic dried marjoram, crushed between your fingers

¼ teaspoon organic ground cloves

1 teaspoon coarse unrefined sea salt, crushed

½ teaspoon freshly ground organic black pepper

2 cups good homemade broth, such as *Beef Broth* (page 45)

1¼ cups organic buckwheat flour

2 tablespoons pastured butter for cooking

1. Melt the butter over medium heat in a cast iron frying pan. When the butter is hot and bubbly, add the onions and sauté gently for 10 minutes, or until the onions have softened.

2. Remove the sausage from its skin, and break it up with a fork in a bowl. Add the sausage to the pan. Add the marjoram, cloves, salt, and pepper. Add the broth.

3. Bring the mixture to a boil. Add the buckwheat flour gradually, stirring constantly. Set the heat to medium and cook for 10 minutes, stirring occasionally. The mixture will form into a firm mass.

4. Turn the heat to low, and spread the mixture out evenly over the pan. Let it cook on low heat for 30 minutes.

5. Place the mixture into a bowl, level the top, and let it sit until cool. Remove from the bowl onto a board and cut into ½ inch slices.

6. Heat the butter in a cast iron frying pan over medium heat. When the butter is hot and bubbly, cook each slice for 2 minutes on each side.

Serve and enjoy.

Marinades

Old California Marinade

About Marinades, or
Why My Marinades are Different

There has been a long-standing debate on the effect of marinades on meat. Some cooking authorities insist that marinades tenderize meat, while others just as vociferously claim that marinades do nothing to tenderize meat, and only add flavor.

They're both right, and they're both wrong. It depends on the kind of marinade. I have discovered that marinades with a significant amount of acidic ingredients, such as wine, vinegar, or lemon juice, do not make grassfed meat more tender. But marinades that are based on the right kind of oil greatly increase the tenderness of the meat. I have also discovered that certain vegetables, when properly crushed, can tenderize meat, without any oil, wine, or vinegar.

Acidic marinades can actually make grassfed meat tougher. Oil-based marinades make grassfed meat more tender. The major reason for this is moisture and liquid. Cooking steaks and roasts is a dry heat process which uses some fat to lubricate the meat. Acidic ingredients such as wine, vinegar, and fruit juice make the meat moist and wet. Even if you wipe the acidic marinade off the meat, some of the liquid in the meat will seep out and interfere with the cooking process.

An oil-based marinade does not make the meat moist and wet, instead the oil lubricates it. Meat is best cooked dry and well lubricated.

I have also discovered some tenderizing vegetable marinades that do not make the meat wet, and do not interfere with the cooking process. This may be because of the relatively small amount of liquid that is released from the crushed vegetables as juices, and because part of what is released is the essential oil of the vegetable.

I now believe that the real purpose of acidic ingredients in marinades was to preserve meat in the days before refrigeration. I have also found that acidic ingredients change the taste and texture of the meat. When cooking steaks or roasts, I prefer to highlight and bring out the natural flavor of the meat, rather than change it too much.

Occasionally, I do use some lemon juice, always combined with a much larger amount of oil. I will also use marinades with a small amount of acidic ingredients for lamb, as I like those changes in taste and texture.

Remember, the use of unfiltered extra virgin olive oil will tenderize meat without any need for acidic ingredients. This kind of olive oil not only lubricates the meat, but tenderizes it.

Tips for Oil-Based Marinades

Many of the recipes in this book use the same marinating process.

- The meat is coated with an oil-based marinade and placed in a covered container. It then stays at room temperature for 1 hour. This initial marination period at room temperature is important. Oil-based marinades will not penetrate the meat if immediately refrigerated, because the oil will cool and solidify.

- The meat is then put in the refrigerator. By this time, the oil has penetrated into the meat, and most of it will stay there. The meat is usually refrigerated overnight.

- If you want to marinate the meat on the same day you cook it, you can skip the refrigeration, and marinate the meat at room temperature for 2 hours or more.

- At least 1 hour before cooking, the meat is removed from the refrigerator, so it can come to room temperature before cooking.

- Many recipes instruct you to scrape the marinade off with a spoon. This is important because you don't want too much between the meat and the heat.

- The best container for a marinade is a glass or ceramic bowl not much larger than the meat you are putting inside. While plastic freezer bags are convenient, there is a concern about chemicals from the plastic being drawn into the food, especially if the marinade ingredients interact with the plastic. This can affect the taste of the meat. Some plastic bags are better than others. One way to minimize any interaction with plastic is to wrap the marinated meat in natural wax paper before placing it in the plastic bag.

- Do not add salt to the marinade for grassfed meat. I have found that pre-salting grassfed meat for an extended period of time can really toughen it. Salt, however, can really bring out the flavors of a dish. Salting the meat just before cooking does not toughen it. The salt in fish sauce, which is a fermented sauce, does not toughen meat.

About Tenderizing Vegetable Marinades

Not everybody wants to use oil to marinate meat. You can tenderize grassfed meat without any oil, wine, or vinegar. You just need the right vegetables.

The trick is to get the vegetable juices out of the vegetable so the juices will penetrate the meat, and tenderize it. I do not advocate the use of juicers or food processors for this purpose, as these high speed machines change the taste and effect of the marinade. However, using a good blender on the lowest speed works well.

Traditionally, vegetables were crushed with kitchen tools. Crush the vegetables with a heavy tool like a rolling pin, cleaver, or heavy bladed knife. Crushing the vegetables causes the natural juices and oils to slowly seep out. They penetrate the meat beautifully, making the meat tender and delicious. I have chosen traditional combinations of ingredients which have been used to flavor meat for hundreds of years. The results are so delicious that I use these marinades for the wonderful taste they impart to meat.

Secret Seasoning Salt

This salt is quite different from the usual seasoning salts which are made with dry ingredients. It has a fresh, aromatic quality that really enhances the flavor of grassfed meat. The secret to this salt is that everything in it is fresh and organic, except for the actual salt itself. Only coarse, unrefined sea salt should be used in this recipe. I make this salt in small batches, and keep it refrigerated. The herbs and garlic permeate the coarse grains of salt, and create a terrific flavor combination.

> 2 tablespoons coarse unrefined sea salt
> 2 teaspoons fresh organic thyme leaves, finely chopped
> 1 teaspoon fresh organic rosemary leaves, finely chopped
> 1 teaspoon fresh organic parsley leaves, finely chopped
> 1 teaspoon fresh organic sage leaves, finely chopped
> 1 teaspoon organic chives, (or organic green onion tops), finely chopped
> 2 large organic garlic cloves, very finely chopped

1. Mix all the ingredients together, making sure they are mixed well, and place in a small jar. Close the jar, and refrigerate.

When using this seasoning salt, remove from the jar what you need, and crush it with a rolling pin, just before use. This final crushing really blends the flavors. *Secret Seasoning Salt* gives great flavor to any meat.

Tenderizing Olive Oil Marinade

This is one of the easiest marinades you will ever make. It is also one of the most effective marinades you will ever use. It has one ingredient. Just one. Unfiltered, organic, extra virgin olive oil.

The discovery of this marinade gave me the ability to make tender grassfed meat. The discovery itself hinged on a moment of inspiration. My research had come across many references to brushing meat with olive oil before cooking, to tenderize the meat. A friend of mine came back from Argentina, and raved about the tender meat there, which was grassfed. He told me it was common for Argentines to coat newly bought meat with oil before refrigerating it. I tried coating grassfed meat with oil. I tried peanut oil, grapeseed oil, extra virgin olive oil. None of these tenderized the meat. I stopped trying.

A few days later, I was reading an article by Sally Fallon in which she talked about how olive oil used to be cloudy before it was filtered, and about how the unfiltered oil was full of enzymes and lipids that were removed by the filtering process. ENZYMES? The realization came to me that I had only used filtered oil with no enzymes. I realized that traditional oil would have been unfiltered! I went down to my local Whole Foods, and found a bottle of unfiltered organic extra virgin olive oil. Appropriately enough, the oil was from Argentina. I coated a grassfed steak, let it rest at room temperature for a couple of hours, then sautéed it. Tender, tender, tender, with the rich beefy flavor of the meat coming out as it never had before. I had found it!

I have since discovered several other ways of making tender grassfed meat. This method still works like a charm. It is great for beef, bison, and lamb.

The trick is to use the right oil, use the right amount, and give the oil some time to penetrate the meat before refrigerating it.

The oil must be organic, unfiltered, and extra virgin. The right amount is just enough to coat all surfaces of the meat. If you drown the meat in the oil, it will have a strong olive flavor. If you use just enough to coat it, it will be really tender, and the natural flavor of the meat will come out. The amount of oil given in the recipes is the right amount. The meat should sit at room temperature for about an hour before refrigerating, so the oil can penetrate the meat instead of congealing on the surface.

The Right Amount

2 tablespoons unfiltered organic extra virgin olive oil, (or enough to coat the meat)

1. Rub the oil into the meat, coating all surfaces.

2. Let it sit at room temperature for 1 hour, then cover and refrigerate overnight. (Alternatively, you can let it sit at room temperature for 2 hours, then cook.)

Old California Marinade

Cattle was king in old California, before gold was discovered. While leather was the main product, the ranchers ate plenty of beef, all of it grassfed. The flavors in this recipe are based on some ideas I got from my research, with the addition of unfiltered extra virgin olive oil. The flavors may or may not be authentic, but they sure are delicious.

4 cloves organic garlic, finely chopped

2 tablespoons fresh organic oregano, minced

½ teaspoon smoked Spanish paprika, (or 1 teaspoon sweet Spanish paprika)

½ teaspoon freshly ground organic black pepper

3 tablespoons unfiltered organic extra virgin olive oil

1. Mix all ingredients together for a delicious marinade, great for all beef. See recipe on page 64.

Traditional Chinese Flavor Tenderizing Marinade

The combination of garlic, ginger, and green onions is a classic flavor base for all kinds of Chinese dishes. Since I know that ginger has a strong tenderizing effect, I decided to try this combination as the base of a vegetable marinade. This marinade really enhances the flavor of grassfed meat, without overwhelming it. The ginger really tenderizes the meat. This can get the meat tender in just a couple of hours at room temperature, instead of the usual overnight refrigeration.

3 organic green onions, coarsely chopped, and crushed

4 large cloves of organic garlic, coarsely chopped, and crushed

4 teaspoons fresh organic ginger, coarsely chopped, and crushed

1. Crush the vegetables. Mix well, and rub all over the meat. Cover and refrigerate overnight, (or 2 hours at room temperature).

2. If you refrigerated the meat, take it out of the refrigerator 1 hour before you plan to cook it, so it can reach room temperature.

3. Once the meat has reached room temperature, scrape the marinade off. Now you're ready to cook.

Tenderizing Marinade with French Flavors

This marinade includes some vegetables and herbs which have been traditionally used to flavor meat in France. There are many other French flavors, but I particularly like this combination, which includes the flavors of the traditional Bouquet Garni. This marinade will tenderize your grassfed meat, and give it a magnificent French flavor.

1 small organic onion, coarsely chopped
1 large stalk organic celery, coarsely chopped
1 large organic carrot, coarsely chopped
2 cloves organic garlic, finely chopped
2 imported bay leaves, crushed
1 teaspoon fresh organic thyme leaves, finely chopped
6 sprigs organic Italian parsley, chopped
½ teaspoon freshly ground organic black pepper

1. Crush the vegetables. Mix well, and rub all over the meat. Sprinkle the pepper all over the meat. Cover and refrigerate overnight.

2. Take the meat out of the refrigerator 1 hour before you plan to cook it, so it can reach room temperature.

3. Once the meat has reached room temperature, scrape the marinade off. Now you're ready to cook.

Tenderizing Marinade with Italian Flavors

Italian cooking is one of the glories of this planet. The Italians really know how to create flavor. This tenderizing vegetable marinade combines some of the ingredients that have been traditionally used to flavor meat in Italy. The fact that there is some similarity to the French and Polish marinades is no accident. Italian cooks were imported to both nations in Renaissance times, and changed the cuisines of both nations. This recipe will tenderize your meat, and give it a great flavor.

1 medium organic onion, coarsely chopped
1 medium organic carrot, coarsely chopped
1 medium organic celery stalk, coarsely chopped
4 cloves organic garlic, finely chopped
Leaves from one large sprig of organic rosemary, finely chopped

1. Crush the vegetables, and mix well with the rosemary. Rub all over the meat. Cover and refrigerate overnight.

2. Take the meat out of the refrigerator 1 hour before you plan to cook it, so it can reach room temperature.

3. Once the meat has reached room temperature, scrape the marinade off. Now you're ready to cook.

Tenderizing Marinade with Polish Flavors

The magnificent traditional cuisine of Poland has used vegetables in marinades to tenderize beef and other meats. This recipe combines and updates several traditional flavor combinations to create a marinade that will make meat tender and absolutely delicious.

1 medium organic onion, coarsely chopped
1 stalk of organic celery, coarsely chopped
1 small organic carrot, coarsely chopped
10 leafy stalks organic Italian parsley, coarsely chopped
2 tablespoons organic celery leaves, finely chopped
½ teaspoon freshly ground organic black pepper

1. Crush the vegetables. Mix well, and rub all over the meat. Sprinkle the pepper all over the meat. Cover and refrigerate overnight.

2. Take the meat out of the refrigerator 1 hour before you plan to cook it, so it can reach room temperature.

3. Once the meat has reached room temperature, scrape the marinade off. Now you're ready to cook.

Tenderizing Marinade with German Flavors

Americans usually do not think of Germany when they think of great beef. Germans, however, have prized beef from the earliest times, believing that beef gives strength. When it comes to grassfed beef, I agree. The Hunsruck region of Germany is known for its barbecue, which often means beef. The tradition was started when a number of Germans went to South America to work in the late 19th century, where they sampled South American barbecue. When the workers returned to Germany, they had acquired a taste for barbecue. Many of them returned to the Hunsruck region, where they started a tradition of barbecuing meat. There is an annual barbecue competition in Hunsruck, where much meat is soaked in secret marinades, and grilled. It occurred to me that some of these secret marinades might have good flavor. I was unable to acquire any recipes, but I did get a good idea of which ingredients are commonly used, and created this tenderizing vegetable marinade. This marinade really brings out the flavor of grassfed meat, and tenderizes it.

1 small organic onion, coarsely chopped

2 cloves organic garlic, coarsely chopped

8 stalks organic Italian parsley, coarsely chopped

1 teaspoon organic black pepper, freshly ground

1 teaspoon organic thyme leaves, finely chopped

1. Crush the vegetables, and mix well with the pepper and thyme. Rub all over the meat. Cover and refrigerate overnight.

2. Take the meat out of the refrigerator 1 hour before you plan to cook it, so it can reach room temperature.

3. Once the meat has reached room temperature, scrape the marinade off. Now you're ready to cook.

Side Dishes

Pan Roasted Potatoes

This is one of my teenage son's favorite side dishes. Here simple is better than good. Just potatoes cooked in the same pan with a beef roast. The drippings cook right into the potatoes. Imagine potatoes crusty on the outside, soft on the inside, with a wonderful caramelized flavor from the pan juices and the drippings. The main problem is that it is impossible to make enough of them, even in a big roasting pan.

You can make these potatoes with just about any beef roast in this book. Beef tallow is the perfect cooking medium, giving the potatoes a nutty, almost sweet flavor when combined with the juices from the roast. You could substitute pastured butter, natural pork lard, or even olive oil — all are delicious alternatives. But for this dish, beef fat is in a class by itself.

These potatoes can be cooked with any beef roast recipe that starts with a temperature of 400 degrees or more. It's fine if the recipe calls for turning down the temperature at a later stage in the cooking.

Many, many organic potatoes

4 tablespoons grassfed beef tallow, (or grassfed beef suet), shaved or crumbled, (or substitute 4 tablespoons butter, pork lard, or olive oil)

1. Peel the potatoes, and cut each potato into 3 to 6 circular pieces, depending on the size of the potato.

2. Place the beef tallow (or other fat) evenly in the roasting pan, leaving enough room in the middle of the pan for the roast. Place the pan in the oven while you are preheating the oven. Remove the pan from the oven once the fat has melted. There should be enough melted fat to cover the bottom of the pan.

3. After you place the roast in the center of the pan, surround it with the potato slices. Lay each potato slice flat in the pan. The slices should not touch each other, but they can be very close together. Since beef fat has a tendency to cool quickly, move the potatoes around a little with a fork to make sure they are not sticking to the pan.

4. Turn the potatoes over each time you adjust the temperature and/or baste the roast.

Very simple, and very delicious.

Paprika Potatoes in the Style of Argentina

The ranchers of Argentina raise some of the best beef in the world. The cattle are traditionally grassfed and grass finished, growing healthy and tender on the rich grasses of the Pampas, the magnificent grasslands of Argentina. Argentines cook some of the tastiest beef in the world. I have learned a lot from studying Argentine cooking methods, and this knowledge is reflected in this book. Of course, every great piece of beef needs a great side dish to keep it company, and Argentines have come up with some winners. This is my version of one of the most classic Argentine side dishes, potatoes roasted with paprika. The combination of natural sea salt, great paprika, and wonderful olive oil, results in potatoes that go well with every kind of meat. My teenage son likes these so much that he learned how to cook them, just so we could have them more often.

Serves 3 to 6 as a side dish

6 long organic potatoes, medium sized

¼ cup unfiltered organic extra virgin olive oil, preferably from Argentina

1½ teaspoons sweet (dulce) paprika, preferably Pimenton de la Vera brand from Spain, (or organic paprika)

1½ teaspoons coarse unrefined sea salt, crushed

1. Mix the olive oil, paprika, and salt together to make a marinade. Place the marinade in a bowl big enough to hold the potatoes.

2. Put the oven rack at the 2nd lowest position. Preheat the oven to 375 degrees. Peel the potatoes, rinse them with water, and dry them with a towel.

3. Cut each potato into 3 long pieces. Cut each of these pieces in half lengthwise. The final result should be 6 long pieces of roughly equal width.

4. Put the potatoes in the bowl with the marinade, and mix well, so every piece is coated with the marinade.

5. Place the potatoes in a single layer in a greased roasting pan. When the oven has preheated, place the roasting pan in the middle of the oven, and bake for 22 minutes.

6. Remove the potatoes from the oven, turn them over, and return them to the oven. Cook for another 22 minutes.

Remove from the oven and serve hot. They will go wonderfully with your grassfed meat.

Old Fashioned French Fries

It is said that French fries were introduced to America by soldiers who had sampled them in France during World War I. They have become a staple of the fast food industry, which is a shame. The fast food versions use all kinds of artificial ingredients. The potatoes are fried in cheap, modern vegetable oils to produce a product that just does not taste good.

But these French fries are quite different. They are cooked at a lower temperature, and pick up wonderful flavor from the beef tallow. After eating these, you will understand why those soldiers brought this dish back home.

Serves 4 as a side dish

5 medium sized organic russet potatoes, peeled, and cut into small French fry pieces of roughly equal size

Enough beef tallow to provide a 1 inch depth of fat in a high sided frying pan, or cast iron casserole

1. It is important to use the right equipment, and to be careful. You will be working with boiling oil, and you must give this process your undivided attention. Be sure to use a deep sided cast iron frying pan, or a cast iron casserole. You could use stainless steel, but cast iron is best. You should also use a long handled slotted spoon.

2. Divide the prepared potatoes into three equal piles. Melt the beef tallow in the frying pan over medium heat. You want the tallow to be hot, but not too hot. This means that it should bubble freely over the potatoes, but should not scorch them. I always test the temperature of the tallow by putting in one piece of potato, and watching how it cooks. When the tallow is at the proper bubbling point, add the first batch of potatoes, stirring gently with a slotted spoon to spread them out evenly in the tallow.

3. Let the fries bubble for the next 4 to 5 minutes, until they are lightly colored.

4. Carefully remove the potatoes from the oil with a slotted spoon to a plate. Cook the next two batches the same way.

5. Turn the heat up on the oil, to a spot between medium and high, and return the first batch of potatoes to the oil, again using the slotted spoon to spread them out evenly.

6. The potatoes will brown quickly. Carefully remove them from the oil when they are done to your liking, and put them on a wide, shallow, oven-proof bowl or plate. Keep them warm in a low oven while you prepare the next batch. When the second batch is done to your liking, add it to the first batch in the oven. Finish the final batch the same way.

Serve and enjoy. The beef tallow will give these fries a wonderful flavor that will go perfectly with any steak.

Variation

You can also make excellent French fries by using pork lard instead of beef tallow. You must use unhydrogenated pork lard from properly raised pigs. The taste will be different, but superb.

Olive Fries

Sometimes good recipes appear by accident. I was cutting potatoes for **Paprika Potatoes in the Style of Argentina**. For some unknown reason, I cut the first potato into French fries. Since I couldn't use them in the dish I was making, I put them in a bowl of water, and promptly forgot about them. A few minutes before dinner, I noticed the bowl. I quickly drained the potatoes, dried them, and fried them over medium heat in a small amount of olive oil. They were so wonderful that we now make them regularly.

Each batch serves 1 to 2

For Each Batch

2 large organic potatoes

Cool filtered water

Enough extra virgin olive oil to cover the bottom of a 12 inch cast iron frying pan, with a depth of ⅛ inch

1. Peel the potatoes, cut for French fries, and put all the potatoes you plan to make in a bowl of cool, filtered water. Let sit for 30 minutes.

2. Put ⅛ inch of olive oil in a 12 inch cast iron frying pan over medium heat. Remove the potatoes for the first batch from the water, and dry throughly. When the oil is hot, carefully place the potatoes in the frying pan, and cook over medium heat, turning so both sides of the potatoes cook in the oil. They are ready when they are crisp on both sides. Remove the potatoes to a plate when ready.

3. Repeat Steps 1 and 2 above for each batch, making sure that you have ⅛ inch of olive oil in the pan before you add the next batch.

4. When all the batches are done, return all the potatoes to the pan over low heat, flipping the potatoes with a spatula, so they all get hot.

Serve and enjoy.

Heaven and Earth

This is a variation on a traditional German recipe that combines just three ingredients into a masterpiece. The traditional recipe calls for boiling potatoes and apples together in small pieces, and then covering them with freshly cooked bacon.

My variation departs from the traditional by mashing the cooked apple and potato pieces together so they are well combined, and then frying them together in bacon fat. Everyone who has tried it this way has liked it better. The taste is heavenly.

Serves 4 as a side dish

2 pounds of organic potatoes, peeled and quartered

2 large, firm, juicy, organic apples, such as Fuji, peeled and cut into 1 inch pieces

4 slices fat, traditionally made bacon

1. Place the bacon in a cast iron frying pan. Cook the bacon on medium heat, turning as necessary, until it has rendered all its fat. Remove the bacon from the pan, and turn off the heat, leaving the fat in the pan.

2. Bring several quarts of water to a boil. Put the potatoes into the boiling water, and keep at a steady boil for 10 minutes. Add the apples to the potatoes, bring back to a steady boil, and boil for another 10 minutes.

3. Drain the potatoes and apples. Place them in a large bowl. Using a potato masher, or a heavy wooden spoon, mash the potatoes and apples into each other until they are well mixed. You will still have some distinct pieces of apple and potato, but they should all be together in one mass.

4. Crumble the reserved bacon, and mix it into the potato-apple mixture.

5. Heat the bacon fat over medium heat until it is hot. Place the potato-apple mass right into the pan, carefully pressing it into the bacon fat. Cook for 2 minutes over medium heat. Turn the potatoes and apples over, press into the fat with a spoon, and cook for another 2 minutes. Stir the mass with a spoon, moving it around, mixing well. Continue cooking, stirring occasionally, until the mass has become lightly browned. This should take no more than 3 to 4 minutes.

Remove, and serve. Get ready for a taste of heaven.

My Temptation

This is absolutely delicious! Potatoes, creamy milk and butter, sautéed onions, and bacon, baked together until they blend into something wonderful.

This dish was inspired by an old Scandinavian dish called Jansson's Temptation. I say "Scandinavian," because the Danes, Swedes, and Finns all call it their own. Jansson was said to be a fire and brimstone preacher, who denounced every form of fun, including good food. He was caught eating a rich dish of potatoes, cream, onions, and anchovies, which was so good that it tempted him to betray his own principles.

I have made several variations on this dish. All were good, but none were wonderful. Until now.

While no Scandinavian would recognize this as Jansson's Temptation (without the anchovies), Jansson himself would be tempted by this one.

Serves 4 as a side dish

2 tablespoons pastured butter

1 large organic onion, sliced

6 medium organic potatoes, sliced thin, then cut into small thin pieces, approximately 2 inches long and ¼ inch thick

2 large slices of fat natural bacon, either pork or beef, cut into small cubes

1½ cups organic cream, (or half and half), divided into 2 equal (¾ cup) portions

1 tablespoon pastured butter, cut into tiny cubes

1. Melt the butter over medium heat in a heavy bottomed frying pan. When the butter is hot and bubbly, add the onions, and cook for about 5 minutes, or until the onions are soft.

2. Preheat the oven to 400 degrees. Place half the potatoes on the bottom of a greased, medium sized glass baking dish. Place the onions over the potatoes. Place the bacon cubes on top of the onions. Place the rest of the potatoes on top of the bacon. Pour ¾ cup of the cream over the mixture. Sprinkle the tiny cubes of butter over the top.

3. Bake at 400 degrees for 20 minutes.

4. Add the rest (¾ cup) of the cream to the dish, return to the oven, and bake for another 20 minutes.

Serve and enjoy.

Anchovy Variation

The traditional version calls for Swedish anchovies. You can use 12 anchovy fillets instead of the bacon. Just scatter the fillets over the onion layer.

Parsley Potatoes

This dish is a great side for any meat. It is full of parsley which combines with the onion and butter to create a delectable potato dish.

Serves 4 as a side dish

6 organic medium russet potatoes, peeled and quartered
2 teaspoons coarse unrefined sea salt
Leaves from 1 bunch of organic Italian parsley, finely chopped
1 large organic onion, finely chopped
4 tablespoons pastured butter, softened, (or unhydrogenated lard)

1. Bring a pot of water to a boil, and add the salt. Make sure there is enough water to cover the potatoes.

2. When the water is boiling rapidly, add the potatoes, bring back to a boil, and boil steadily for 10 minutes. Drain the potatoes, and place them in a large bowl.

3. Preheat the oven to 400 degrees. Add the parsley and onion to the potatoes, and mix well with a large spoon. The potatoes should break up during the mixing process.

4. Rub half of the butter (or lard) along the bottom and sides of a casserole (cast iron or glass), coating it well. Add the potato mixture to the buttered casserole. Dot the top with the remaining butter, pushing some of the butter deep into the mixture with a spoon.

5. Bake uncovered at 400 degrees for 30 minutes.

Serve and enjoy with your grassfed meat.

Garlic Parsley Potato Casserole
with Spanish Flavors

Garlic and parsley are loaded with health-giving nutrients, and combine wonderfully with each other. Potatoes are very popular in my household, and I wanted a potato dish that would feature lots of garlic and parsley. Since these ingredients are combined quite often in Spanish dishes, I decided to add other Spanish flavors to the mix. The results were tasty and terrific. If you are not a true garlic lover, you may want to halve the amount of garlic. If you like garlic, use the full amount. You'll love the taste, and your body will love the healthy qualities of this delicious dish.

Serves 4 as a side dish

3 pounds organic potatoes, peeled and cut into 6-10 cubes of roughly equal size

2 tablespoons extra virgin olive oil, preferably Spanish

1 bulb organic garlic, peeled and finely chopped

1 small bunch of organic Italian parsley, finely chopped

2 teaspoons coarse unrefined sea salt, crushed

1 tablespoon sweet Spanish paprika, (or organic paprika)

2 tablespoons pastured butter

1. Bring a pot of water to a boil. Make sure there is enough water to cover the potatoes.

2. Add the potatoes to the boiling water, and cook for 10 minutes. Drain the potatoes.

3. Preheat the oven to 350 degrees. Rub the olive oil all over the sides and bottom of a casserole. Add the potatoes, garlic, parsley, salt, paprika, and butter to the casserole, and mix well with a large spoon. Don't worry if the potatoes crumble or break up.

4. Place the casserole in the oven for 30 minutes.

Serve, and enjoy the wonderful blend of flavors.

Swiss Chard Potatoes

This is a delicious and nutritious side dish for any meat. It is full of Swiss chard which combines with the onion and butter to create a potato dish that is unusual and appetizing, with a distinctive flavor imparted by the Swiss chard. It is important that the Swiss chard leaves be very finely chopped. Be sure to leave out the white stems.

Serves 4 as a side dish

6 medium organic russet potatoes, peeled and quartered

2 teaspoons coarse unrefined sea salt, crushed

Green leaves from 1 bunch of organic Swiss chard, very finely chopped

½ cup good homemade bone broth, such as *Chicken* or *Nomad's Broth* (pages 45 - 53)

1 medium organic onion, finely chopped

4 tablespoons pastured butter, softened

1. Bring a pot of water to a boil, and add the salt. Make sure there is enough water to cover the potatoes.

2. When the water is boiling rapidly, add the potatoes, bring back to a boil, and boil steadily for 10 minutes. Drain the potatoes, and place them in a large bowl.

3. Preheat the oven to 400 degrees. Add the Swiss chard leaves, broth, and onion to the potatoes, and mix well with a large spoon. The potatoes should break up during the mixing process. Mix thoroughly.

4. Rub half of the butter along the bottom and sides of a casserole (cast iron or glass), coating it well. Add the potato mixture to the buttered casserole. Dot the top with the remaining butter, pushing some of the butter deep into the mixture with a spoon.

5. Bake uncovered at 400 degrees for 30 minutes.

Serve and enjoy with your grassfed meat.

Onion Cabbage

You only need a few ingredients, if the quality is great. This recipe has only three ingredients, but they combine perfectly to create a masterpiece of caramelized healthy goodness. This is a great side dish for any meat.

Serves 4 as a side dish

3 tablespoons pastured butter
1 large organic onion, sliced
½ medium organic cabbage, sliced

1. Melt the butter in a cast iron frying pan over medium heat. When the butter is hot and bubbly, add all the vegetables.

2. Cook over medium heat, stirring occasionally, until the vegetables have cooked down, and are nicely caramelized without being burned. Feel free to reduce the heat during the later cooking stage to avoid burning.

Serve and enjoy.

European Cabbage

This is one of my favorite side dishes. The caramelized sweetness of this dish tastes terrific. It goes particularly well with beef. Cabbage is one of the most European of vegetables. This dish combines elements of German, French, and Polish cooking so that the ingredients simply blend perfectly.

Serves 4 as a side dish

4 slices fat, traditionally made bacon, (or ¼ cup pastured butter)
1 large organic yellow onion
1 small organic green cabbage
1 large organic apple

1. Place the bacon slices in a cold, 12 inch cast iron frying pan. Turn the heat to medium. The goal is to render the fat from the bacon. Turn the bacon from time to time.

2. Cut the onions into slices. Chop and slice the cabbage. Peel the apples, and cut into small slices.

3. When the bacon has rendered all its fat, add all the other ingredients. (If you are using butter, melt over medium heat until bubbly, and then add the other ingredients.)

4. Cook over medium heat for 10 minutes, stirring occasionally to make sure that the ingredients are well mixed, and to avoid burning.

5. Turn the heat down to medium low, and cook for another 10 minutes, or until the ingredients have shrunk considerably, have browned somewhat, and have melded together in a nice mass. They should be soft and sweet, and have a beautiful blended taste.

Serve with any meat.

Quick Cooked Greens

Green leafy vegetables are known for their health-giving qualities. If organic, they're full of life-giving nutrients, and help balance a meal. Their reputation for being healthy is matched or surpassed by their reputation for tasting terrible, which is undeserved. Greens, if properly cooked, can be absolutely delicious. It is traditional in Southern Europe to cook leafy greens quickly in olive oil and garlic. While other recipes might add other ingredients, I like the basic combination of olive oil, garlic, and greens the best. This recipe reminds us that traditional recipes stand the test of time for a reason — their good taste.

Serves 4 as a side dish

1 bunch organic green leafy vegetables, such as beet greens, or any color chard
¼ cup extra virgin olive oil
4 cloves organic garlic, finely chopped

1. Wash the greens, dry them, and remove the leaves from the stems. Tear the leaves into small to medium pieces.

2. Place the olive oil and garlic together in a 12 inch cast iron frying pan. Heat the pan until the oil is hot, over medium high heat. As soon as the oil is hot, add the leaves. Don't be concerned if it seems that the leaves are overflowing your pan, because they will shrink considerably.

3. Using a long spoon, stir the leaves as they cook. They will shrink considerably, and they may give off some water. Keep stirring and cooking until the water cooks off, the leaves have shrunk considerably, and they take a deep green and slightly brown appearance. This can happen very quickly, within 2 to 3 minutes, so give the pan your constant attention.

4. Once the greens have cooked down, remove the pan from the heat, and give the greens a good stir.

The olive oil, greens, and garlic combine for a wonderful taste and texture.

Roman Asparagus

The ancient Romans not only loved elaborate dishes, but simple ones as well, as long as they were superb. Asparagus may have been the favorite Roman vegetable. The Romans believed in cooking it quickly and simply, and considered overcooked asparagus to be an abomination. The favorite expression of the Roman Emperor Claudius was, "As quick as boiled asparagus!" Boiling vegetables has fallen out of favor in modern times because of the supposed loss of nutrients. Steaming is often recommended. Quickly boiled vegetables retain most of their nutrients, turn a beautiful color, and taste great. The secret is to have some good natural fat in the water, preferably butter.

If you take the Romans' advice on how to cook asparagus, you'll find that it is excellent.

Serves 4 as a side dish

1 pound organic asparagus, with the tough ends trimmed off, cut into 2 inch pieces
2 tablespoons pastured butter
1 quart filtered water

1. Place the butter with 1 quart filtered water in a pot, and bring to a rapid boil over high heat.

2. Dump all of the asparagus at once into the boiling water, being careful not to burn yourself.

3. When the water returns to a boil, remove the pot from the heat, and quickly remove the asparagus with a slotted spoon.

The asparagus will be crisp, tender, and delicious.

Quick Boiled Green Beans

Like asparagus, the cooking of green beans should be short, fast, and intense. The butter makes the difference. Green beans cooked this way are intensely green, crisp, and utterly delicious. While any organic green bean will do, organic Blue Lake green beans are particularly good.

Serves 4 as a side dish

1 pound organic green beans (preferably Blue Lake), tips removed
2 tablespoons pastured butter
1 quart filtered water
1 teaspoon unrefined sea salt

1. Place the butter with 1 quart filtered water in a pot, and bring to a rapid boil over high heat. Add the salt.

2. When the water has reached a strong boil, add the beans. Let the water come back to a boil, and cook for 1 to 2 minutes until the beans are very green. Drain the beans, dress with some more butter, and enjoy.

Quick, Delicious Broccoli

Broccoli has long been known as one of the healthiest vegetables. It is also one of the most hated vegetables, when badly cooked. Properly cooked broccoli is wonderful. Once again, the key is quick cooking and good butter. The butter brings out the sweet, green flavor of organic broccoli. The quick cooking locks in the flavor, and creates a crisp texture that is a joy to bite into.

Serves 4 as a side dish

1 pound organic broccoli florets, cut into 1 inch pieces
3 tablespoons pastured butter
1 quart filtered water

1. Place the butter with 1 quart filtered water in a pot, and bring to a rapid boil over high heat.

2. Dump all of the broccoli at once into the boiling water, being careful not to burn yourself.

3. When the water returns to a boil, let the broccoli boil for 1 minute. Remove the pot from the heat, and quickly remove the broccoli with a slotted spoon.

This broccoli will actually be delicious.

Cheese with Eggs

This is a great side dish for people who wish to avoid carbohydrates, but want something tasty to go with their grassfed meat. Actually, this is a great side dish for anybody.

Cheese made from raw milk has great flavor, but you could use any good natural cheese. The large amount of cheese melts right into the eggs, blending into a delicious whole. In fact, it is a little like a cheese sauce. Meat and melted cheese are great together.

Serves 4 as a side dish

4 organic eggs, preferably from free range chickens
1 tablespoon filtered water
1 cup crumbled cheese, preferably raw milk cheddar
2 tablespoons pastured butter

1. Beat the eggs with the water until they are well mixed.

2. Mix the cheese with the eggs and water.

3. Melt the butter in a heavy bottomed pan over medium heat.

4. When the butter is hot and bubbly, add the mixture and cook, stirring constantly until the cheese has melted, which should happen quickly.

Serve and enjoy.

Blue Cheese Omelet with Spanish Flavor

One of the most famous Spanish steak dishes is served with a sauce based on blue cheese, usually the excellent Cabrales. That sauce served as the inspiration for this omelet, which makes a delicious low-carb side dish. The combination of steak and melted blue cheese is just wonderful, and the omelet is a great vehicle for the blue cheese.

Serves 4 as a side dish

4 large organic eggs

1 organic garlic clove, finely chopped

½ teaspoon organic sweet Spanish paprika

½ cup imported blue cheese, such as Cabrales, Roquefort, or Danish blue cheese, crumbled

2 tablespoons extra virgin olive oil, (preferably Spanish)

1. Combine all ingredients except the olive oil. Mix well.

2. Heat the olive oil in a heavy bottomed pan over medium heat. When the oil is hot, pour in the mixture. Let it cook until the cheese has melted. Serve immediately.

Appendix

Finding and Purchasing Grassfed Meat

Most supermarkets do not carry grassfed and grass finished meat. This leaves you with the option of buying from a local rancher, or buying from the Internet. Here are some tips:

The Definition of Grassfed Meat Is Vague and Confusing

Since all cattle, bison, and sheep are fed grass at some time in their life, you could argue that all cattle, bison, and sheep are "grassfed." True grassfed meat comes only from animals that have been fed and finished on grass.

The animals should be fed the grasses and legumes they find in the pasture, and that's it. No grains, no soy, no animal by-products, no "rendered" products, nothing but the grasses and legumes growing in the pasture. An exception must be made for the winter months in certain parts of the country, when the animals are fed hay, dried grass, and sometimes silage (fermented grass). This was traditionally done in winter.

Make sure that the producer does not use any hormones, growth promotants, or subtherapeutic antibiotics. Many people believe that no animal that has ever been treated with antibiotics should be eaten. The decision is yours, once you know the antibiotic policy of the producer.

The producer's website usually contains a lot of information on these issues. Review these articles to be sure that the meat is really grassfed and grass finished. If you have any doubt, don't hesitate to call and ask. If you are buying from a local rancher or market, talk with them.

Don't accept anything less than a clear answer. After all, the questions — what food and drugs are given to the animals — are very simple.

Deceptive Advertising Is Used by Some Meat Producers

The terms "all natural," "natural," "free range," and "organic" do not mean that the meat is grassfed and grass finished. In fact, most of the meat produced with these descriptions is grain finished.

The Taste of Grassfed Meat Varies Greatly

This is inevitable. Because of the very nature of grassfed meat, the taste of the meat will depend on what grasses are eaten by the animal. Since different varieties of grass grow all over the country, the meat from different producers will have a different flavor. In fact, even the meat from the same producer may taste a little different at various times of the year, because the content of the grasses vary and the animals are usually rotated through different pastures. I have grown to really enjoy these differences, much like a wine enthusiast will enjoy a variety of wines.

In my opinion, grasses in the U.S. give a variety of great tastes to grassfed meat, far better than the grasses in Australia and New Zealand, for example. Grassfed meat has flavor, real flavor, right in the meat. The variety in those flavors is a tasty blessing.

The Aging Process Varies Greatly

Aging is a traditional process which really increases the flavor and tenderness of beef. It used to be that all beef was dry aged, which meant that it was hung in a meat locker under controlled temperature conditions for a certain number of days, commonly twenty-one. The dry aging process required a skilled and experienced butcher. The meat would shrink somewhat during this procedure, losing excess moisture, concentrating the flavor, and becoming much more tender.

Wet aging was introduced some years ago. The meat would be tightly sealed in some sort of plastic, usually Cryovac®, and left to sit in its own juices. The advantage was that the meat did not shrink. Since it did not shrink, it did not develop the concentrated flavor created by dry aging. It did become more tender. Some authorities have stated that wet aging is safer than dry aging, since improper dry aging can result in spoilage. Wet aging quickly became the standard, since it was more profitable, and dry aging became rare.

Some producers dry age their meat, some wet age it for an extended period of time, and some wet age it for a minimal time. I used to believe that only dry aging was acceptable. I changed my mind after having excellent beef that was wet aged for a minimum of thirty days. I was also pleasantly surprised to taste some excellent beef that was minimally aged.

Less Water = More Meat

The per pound price of grassfed meat is almost always higher than other meat of the same cut, sometimes much higher. However, grassfed meat is much denser than factory meat or grain fed meat, which really reduces shrinkage in cooking. I have found that grassfed meat cooked by a dry heat method (grilling, pan broiling, roasting, frying, sautéing) shrinks much less than the other meats. Grassfed meat cooked by a wet heat method (stewing, braising, pot roasting) also shrinks less than the other meat, but the difference is not as great.

Not only does grassfed meat shrink less, grassfed meat is much more satisfying. Less meat is required for a meal if it is grassfed. This can be more economical.

Prices of Various Cuts Differ Greatly

This can take some getting used to. The price per pound for the same cut of meat can be very different, depending on the producer.

The prime cuts such as strip loin, ribeye, and especially tenderloin, can be very expensive. However, these prime cuts are only a small percentage of the animal's weight, and the producer needs to sell the rest of the animal. This means that you can buy some excellent pieces of meat at a much lower price. Cuts such as center cut shoulder, cross rib, and sirloin tip, can make wonderfully tender steaks and roasts, while cuts such as chuck, bottom round, and brisket can make terrific pot roasts and stews. Just about every producer has affordable hamburger, especially when you buy in bulk, and grassfed hamburger is so much better.

Producers often run specials, especially when they are overstocked on a particular cut of meat. You can also save a lot of money by purchasing a discount package, or in bulk. Some producers sell primal cuts, which means you can save as much as 35 to 40 percent if you cut your own steaks and boneless roasts. It is very easy to cut boneless meat, if you have a suitable sharp knife.

Comparing prices can save you a lot of money.

Definitions of Different Cuts of Meat Differ Greatly

This can also lead to confusion. Different parts of the country have different names for the same cut of beef. This is especially true for the term "chuck." Chuck actually consists of several very different cuts of meat, some of which are suitable for dry roasting, and some of which are not. The tender shoulder cuts such as cross rib and center cut shoulder are often called chuck, as are other cuts which are so full of connective tissue that they are suitable only for pot roasts and stews.

Feel free to ask the producer if you are unsure about a particular cut.

Cuts of Meat Available Differ Greatly

Just about everybody carries the prime boneless cuts such as tenderloin, strip loin, and ribeye, and everybody has ground meat. But many other cuts can be hard to find. It can be particularly hard to find bone in steaks or roasts.

If you don't see what you want, ask for it. The producer may be able to get it for you. If not, chances are that somebody else will.

It is not unusual for a producer to run out of a particular cut of meat from time to time. Depending on their protocol for raising and aging the meat, it can take a while until they are restocked. Remember that these are real ranches and farms, not factories.

Shipping Procedures and Costs Differ Greatly

Additional charges for shipping can range from nothing to a lot of money, depending on the producer.

It is important to find out what the shipping charges are before you complete your order, so you will know what it will cost you.

Most producers will ship only on certain days of the week, and some will ship only once or twice a month. It is important to know when the meat will ship and when it will arrive.

Customer Service Differs Greatly

When you are ordering meat through the Internet or mail, mistakes can happen. You can get shipped the wrong cut, the meat can weigh less than it should, or your order may, in rare instances, never arrive. When that happens, customer service becomes crucial. The overwhelming majority of grassfed meat producers that I have dealt with are good, decent, hardworking, and honorable. It is important to remember that their expertise is in raising terrific, healthy, and delicious meat — not slick public relations.

If you do have a problem with an order, I recommend contacting the producer, and describing the problem factually. Most of the producers I have dealt with will make things right, once they understand the problem.

Sources for Grassfed Meat

There are many sources for grassfed meat both locally and on the Internet. You can check out local sources for grassfed meat. Many markets now carry grassfed and grass finished meat, as do some farmers' markets. Make sure that the meat is both grassfed and grass finished.

Here are some of the sources that we use personally. I and my family have eaten the meat of each and every one of these producers, on multiple occasions. None of these producers knew I was writing this book when I first ordered their meat. I consider the meat from each of these producers to be grassfed and grass finished. The meat of each of these producers is excellent, and works with the recipes in this book. All of them are committed to the grassfed movement and believe in what they do. All of them treat their animals with respect and take excellent care of them.

Beef

Alderspring Ranch
www.alderspring.com
May, Idaho
(208) 876-4083

Fox Fire Farms
www.foxfirefarms.com
Ignacio, CO 81137
(970) 563-4675

U.S. Wellness Meats
www.grasslandbeef.com
Monticello, MO 63457
(877) 383-0051

Bison

BisonRidge Ranch
www.bisonridgeranch.com
Montello, Wisconsin 53949
(608) 589-5500

Northstar Bison
www.northstarbison.com
Rice Lake, WI 54868
(715) 234-9085

Lamb

Fox Fire Farms
www.foxfirefarms.com
Ignacio, CO 81137
(970) 563-4675

Northstar Bison
www.northstarbison.com
Rice Lake, WI 54868
(715) 234-9085

U.S. Wellness Meats
www.grasslandbeef.com
Monticello, MO 63457
(877) 383-0051

Index

LaVergne, TN USA
23 December 2009
167901LV00001B/7/P